JEEP
GOES TO WAR

JEEP
GOES TO WAR

WILLIAM FOWLER

PB

PARKGATE
BOOKS

Published in 1998 by Parkgate Books Ltd
Kiln House, 210 New Kings Road
London SW6 4NZ

Produced by PRC Publishing Ltd

ISBN 1 90261 603 0

Printed in China

The right of Will Fowler to be identified as the author
has been asserted by the same in accordance with
the Copyright, Designs and Patents Art 1988.

Dedication
To Catherine, a driving force

PAGE 1: A GI cuts
loose with an M2 .5in
Browning machine
gun mounted on an
M151 in Vietnam.

PAGES 2-3: Men of the
173rd Airborne
Brigade in Vietnam
with a 106mm
recoilless rifle
mounted on an
M151A2.

BELOW: During trials
in the USA a jeep is
driven out of a CG-4A
Waco glider.

BELOW RIGHT: General
Dwight D Eisenhower
rides in General
George S Patton's
jeep. The twin horns
are visible and
general's stars as well
as unit insignia are
attached to the hood.
Mudguards and side
doors have been
fitted.

CHAPTER ONE
THE ORIGINS OF THE JEEP
6

CHAPTER TWO
THE JEEP AT WAR
24

CHAPTER THREE
FIGHTING WITH OUR FRIENDS
50

CHAPTER FOUR
VARIATIONS ON A THEME
68

CHAPTER FIVE
THE JEEP MARCHES ON
80

CHAPTER SIX
THE NEW PRETENDERS
94

INDEX AND ACKNOWLEDGMENTS
111

THE ORIGINS OF THE JEEP

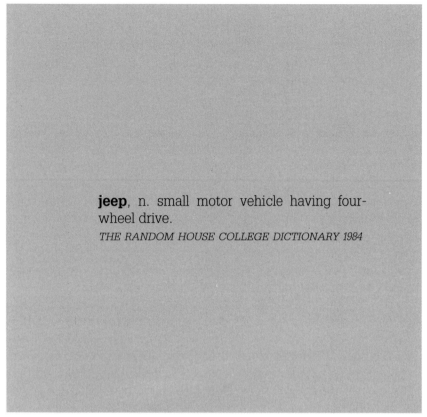

jeep, n. small motor vehicle having four-wheel drive.

THE RANDOM HOUSE COLLEGE DICTIONARY 1984

This brief entry in a dictionary gives little indication of the enormous impact that the compact US 4x4 command reconnaissance vehicle, better known as the jeep, had on World War II and on cross-country vehicle design during the decades following the end of that conflict.

Jeep Goes to War follows the story of the utility vehicle from the early plans for a cross-country military vehicle, through its development and the war years, to the M151 and M38 of the 1960s and their up-to-date cousin, the M998 HMMWV (Humvee) which played an important part in the victory over Iraq in 1991.

It is hard now, looking back, to appreciate the impact that the jeep made when it appeared in large numbers on all fronts in World War II. Though private cars were used in large numbers in the United States before the war, they were very much an expensive luxury in Europe in the 1930s.

Indeed, few people could drive. During the war years, however, Allied soldiers were taught driving skills and grew accustomed to

PREVIOUS PAGES: A beautifully restored Willys jeep in World War II British Airborne forces markings.

LEFT: The AM General Corporation M151A2 4×4 vehicle. The M151 was also known as the MUTT – Military Utility Tactical Truck.

BELOW: Left to right, the Quad, Willys Model MB, M38A1 and M606A2. This line up shows the development of the jeep concept over 20 years.

ABOVE: An LTV HMMWV truck fitted with Stinger anti-aircraft missiles. On the move the missile tubes are folded flat which makes the vehicle look like a conventional cargo carrier.

LEFT: A HMMWV fitted with an M60 machine gun, guards a USAF C-141 Starlifter heavy transport at Dharan in Saudi Arabia, 1990.

ABOVE RIGHT: A British Army Ford GPW fitted for radio and with the mailed fist insignia of the 6th Armoured Division.

RIGHT: A Brockbank cartoon in a wartime edition of Punch features the jeep.

the convenient on-road and cross-country mobility that the jeep offered. In postwar Europe, a car was regarded as essential, particularly by ex-servicemen, many of whom had received their driving instruction at the wheel of the ubiquitous jeep.

The jeep was also regarded with a great deal of affection by many soldiers. A contemporary account from World War II, describing how two correspondents drove from Burma to India in a jeep illustrates the point. When they met an officer and told him about the journey, he as good as intimated that they were liars. "There isn't a single road across these jungles and hills," he protested vehemently. "Sh-h-h! Don't talk so loud," replied one of the correspondents, "Our jeep hasn't found out about roads yet, and we don't want to spoil her!" What then was so special about this vehicle that engendered such humor and obvious affection, and what were its origins?

At the turn of the nineteenth century, shortly after the internal combustion engine had been married to a chassis, gears, transmission, steering and brakes, imaginative soldiers realized that they could combine mobility and firepower to devastating effect. Warfare, which for so long had been based on human muscle and horsepower was changed forever. Many armed forces began to experiment with mobile forces.

In 1904, the French used a modified Panhard car armed with a Hotchkiss machine gun to reconnoiter routes and carry dispatches through hostile territory in North Africa. The conversion work on this four-seater Panhard tourer had been undertaken by a factory in the Rue d'Ivry, Paris, by a Captain Gentil. His was probably the first military reconnaissance/liaison vehicle in the world.

It was World War I that accelerated the demand for field cars. The little Model T Ford, for example, was used by the British for patrol and reconnaissance missions in the Middle East. The bodywork was stripped down, and its crew of four were armed with a Vickers .303in medium machine gun. The Rolls-Royce Tender also used in the Middle East was a larger vehicle approximating to a light truck.

Between the wars, the British Austin Seven, which had been developed as an inexpensive family car, was built under license by BMW in Germany as the Dixi, in the United States by American Austin, and also in Japan. Essentially a two-seater, the Austin

"I suppose you realize you're driving on the wrong side of the road."

Seven was used by the armies of all four countries as a radio reconnaissance and liaison vehicle. Before the Nazi armaments industry got into top gear it gave the modest Reichswehr the first opportunity to experiment with rudimentary Blitzkrieg tactics.

In Europe, the emphasis was on cross-country vehicles, especially tractors for towing anti-tank and light anti-aircraft guns. The British also modified 4x2 saloon tourers for use as military vehicles. In 1939, the Army had a pool of 4285 civilian cars and 3806 War Department (WD) vehicles; by 1940 the figures were 2315 and 12600 respectively. At the close of the war in Europe, the figures had jumped dramatically; there were 134,573 cars in British service. The vehicles varied from almost purely civilian types with a simple camouflage scheme, to more specialized cars with heavy duty bumpers, black-out lights and roof-racks. Many of these latter vehicles were, of course, jeeps. Other European states were also developing lightweight military utility transports.

Before the war, the French vehicle industry produced the V 10M, a compact 4x4 car which was canceled when France surrendered in 1940. The little civilian Simca 5, a French version of the Fiat Topolino, was initially requisitioned by the French Army in

ABOVE: A Luftwaffe officer eats a snack meal by his dusty VW Kubelwagen. His "plate" is a lid from a captured British Army cooking container.

LEFT: Afrika Korps soldiers with an MG34 machine gun in a Kubelwagen. It is fitted with balloon tires and spare petrol "jerrican".

The Kubelwagen

The Kubelwagen was so-called because its seating was of the "Kubel" (bucket) type. Though the correct military designation, l.gl.Pkw Kfz.1, mit Fahrgestell der l.Pkw (o) — (o) indicated that the car or chassis was of a type that was commercially available — it was more commonly known as the Kubelsitzer, Kubelwagen or Kubel. The Kfz 2, 2/40 3 and 4 models were similar to the Kfz 1 but fitted out for more specialized roles.

A typical vehicle, the Kfz.1 (Volkswagen [Kdf] 82)(leichter Personenkraftwagen K1 Type 82), was powered by a VW Type 1, 4-cylinder, H-1-A-R 985cc 24bhp engine rated at 3000rpm (from March 1943: 1131cc, 25bhp rated at 3000rpm). Transmission was 4FIR with limited-slip differential. Brakes were mechanical and for operations in Europe tires were 5.25-16, though in North Africa balloon types were fitted. The wheelbase was 2400mm, which contrasts with the jeep's of 2032mm.

The one vice of the jeep was that its narrow wheelbase could make it unstable at speed. The Kubelwagen was 3740mm long, 1600mm wide and 1650mm high, and weighed 685kg. Interestingly, the prototype of the Kubelwagen was built by a name more commonly associated with luxury cars — Porsche.

Intriguingly, like the American jeep, the design reappeared as a civilian vehicle after the war. The Volkswagen 181 was adopted by the West German army and modified for military use as the Pkw 0.4t. Between 1969 and 1970, 2000 were supplied to the army and other vehicles entered service with the Austrian, Danish, French and Dutch armed forces.

A significant difference between the wartime and postwar designs was that the Pkw 0.4t had a more powerful engine which developed 44bhp at 4000rpm. The front trunk on the postwar vehicle was less sharply angled and so had a larger internal capacity.

Parallels with the development of the US jeep extend to the German amphibious light vehicle. Some 150 Porsche 4x4 amphibious light cars were built for trials in 1940; they were bigger and slightly less powerful than the production Kfz 1/20, K2s VW 166 Schwimmwagen or Kradschutzen Ersatzwagen of which 14,265 were produced. This four-seater, 4x4 vehicle weighed 910kg, was powered by a 4-cylinder, 25bhp, 5FIR engine which powered a hinged three-blade propeller when the Schwimmwagen took to the water. It was capable of 80km/h on roads and 5km/h in water.

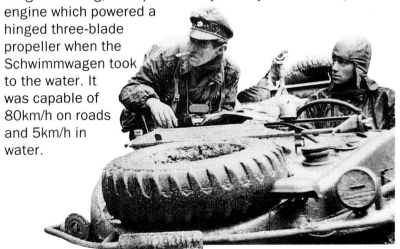

1939, then captured by the Germans in 1940 and later re-captured, or perhaps liberated, by the Allies in 1944-45. The Dutch firm of DAF built a prototype 4x4 amphibian, the MC 139, which, unusually, had driving positions at the front and rear. The engine from a front-wheel drive Citroën was mounted transversely between the front and rear driving positions.

The Italian armed forces were equipped with the 508 C Militare which was based on the Fiat Balilla. Built before the war as a "tourer," it was in effect a pseudo-military vehicle and was known as a "colonial" car. It was powered by a four-cylinder engine which gave 30bhp at 4400rpm, but only had rear-wheel drive. Most colonial cars were built by Fiat, but Alfa Romeo produced the 6C2500 and Bianchi the S4, S6 and S9.

Japan built the Kurogane Type 95, a little 4x4 two-seater known as the Black Medal. It had a two-cylinder engine which developed a modest 25bhp but its fuel consumption was low at about eight liters per 100km. Some 4800 were produced by Kurogane, and other similar petrol and diesel-powered vehicles were built by Toyota and Rikuo. Later in the war, a captured US Bantam jeep was copied by Toyota and five pilot models were produced.

Although these European vehicles were more or less successful, none was a serious competitor to the jeep. Only in Hitler's Germany were there real rivals to the American model. The prewar German automotive industry was one of the most sophisticated in Europe. However, instead of producing a low-cost 4x4 field car, which could have equipped a large army, designs were costly and elaborate.

As Bart H Vanderveen observes in his *Fighting Vehicles Directory of World War II*: "It must have been a paradise for vehicle designers. What other army would produce beautifully designed tourer-type cars with independent suspension and other refinements just to transport four soldiers comfortably with their kit and equipment?" As his excellent guide explains, when the Germans realized that they were in for a long war, they rationalized their models and simplified production. The Volkswagon Kubelwagen, 52,000 of which had been produced by the end of the war, and which has been described as the "German jeep," was a product of the streamlined program.

LEFT: Jeeps on parade in the Middle East. They are towing US supplied 37mm M3A1 anti-tank guns.

BELOW LEFT: A British soldier poses at the wheel of a jeep in the Middle East during World War II. Unlike operational vehicles, this jeep has not been loaded with weapons and equipment.

BELOW: A battered SAS jeep in North Africa, it has three Vickers "K" guns and a Browning .5in machine gun. Fuel and water cans are strapped on and the cut down radiator grill is fitted with a condenser.

While Europe braced itself for war in the late 1930s and looked at various cross-country vehicle designs, the United States was seemingly secure across the Atlantic. Though politicians might have been isolationist, viewing involvement in a future war in Europe with distaste, the military remained realistic. Resources were limited for the interwar US Army, but this did not prevent soldiers and vehicle manufacturers examining requirements for a light, low-cost, cross-country vehicle which could carry small-caliber armament or tow antitank guns or mountain artillery. The jeep would be the product of these deliberations.

It is generally agreed that no single person invented the jeep. Light vehicles had been tested by the US Army as far back as the early 1920s. After the experience of the trenches in World War I, soldiers realized that they needed a carrier which could transport bulky and cumbersome support weapons like medium machine guns and mortars across difficult terrain. Man-packing them left men exhausted and meant that only small amounts of ammunition could be carried.

In 1923, a Model T Ford was stripped down and evaluated by the Ordnance Department. Fitted with rudimentary balloon tires (which were surplus aircraft types), front-wheel drive and a light canvas tilt, this reconnaissance tractor was a distant ancestor of the jeep.

In the early 1930s Arthur W Herrington, Co-President of the Marmon-Herrington Company of Indianapolis embarked on a private venture to fit a Ford 1½ tonner with four-wheel drive. The vehicle proved too heavy, so Herrington worked on a lighter Ford in 1936 and tested it at King Ranch in Texas. Others were also looking at utility vehicles.

In the 1935 issue of the influential *American Cavalry Journal*, Lieutenant H G Hamilton wrote an article entitled "A light cross-country car." It included a line drawing which now looks uncannily like a British Special Air Service (SAS) Regiment jeep from World War II and, indeed, all subsequent 4x4 long-range patrol vehicles. Hamilton's car had two machine guns, bullet-proof glass for the driver's windshield, rations, water and fuel stowed on board and a radio. The young officer had identified the basic requirements,

and proposed a vehicle which could fulfil them.

On June 26 1937 the US Defense Department acquired five Marmon-Herrington Ford 4x4 (Model LD 1) and evaluated them at Fort Bennington, Georgia. Financial backing from Walter C Marmon and concepts developed by Herrington had made the Marmon-Herrington respected military vehicle specialists since its foundation on March 13 1931.

The Army was impressed by the model's low silhouette, 450kg payload and top speed of over 56km/h. On January 20 1939, the depot at Camp Holabird placed an order for 64 of the vehicles. With the benefit of hindsight, the Marmon-Herrington-Ford team would call the vehicle ''The Grand-daddy of the Jeep,'' though its first name was the rather less martial ''Our Darling.''

In early 1937 Major Robert G Howie and Master Sergeant Melvyn C Wiley took the proven Austin Seven engine (supplied by the American Bantam Car Company of Butler, Pennsylvania), and fitted it to a chassis which was less than one meter high. With the engine in the rear and a crew of two who operated the vehicle in a prone position, it was armed with a water-cooled Browning

BELOW: ''Margie'' a US Army jeep in Tunisia; it is loaded with bed rolls, two jerricans, a spare wheel with chains fitted, and a pack with entrenching tool.

ABOVE: A French officer with members of the Resistance at Flers in Normandy in August 1944. The jeep carries five German paratroopers who have been taken prisoner.

.3in machine gun with 1500 rounds. It weighed 460kg had a wheelbase of 1.9m and a top speed of 45km/h.

Howie had hoped that it would be "a snake in the grass." However, when the US Army tested it in April 1937 it earned the less-flattering nickname "Belly Flopper." It also proved to be tiring to drive due to the lack of shock absorbers.

In March 1940, General Walter C Short invited Delmar Ross, Chief Engineer of Willys-Overland Motors Inc of Toledo, Ohio, and Joseph W Frazer, the president of the company, to witness a demonstration of the "Belly Flopper." Ross saw the potential of the flawed design, thereby initiating a further step in the evolution of the jeep.

In 1938 the American Bantam Car Company had lent three standard Austin roadsters to the state's National Guard, which evaluated them during their summer exercises. Charles Payne, who was in charge of Bantam sales to the Army, suggested to the military authorities that there was a considerable potential for a special reconnaissance vehicle based on the roadster.

Payne's idea interested the technical services of the US Army and in June 1940 they laid down their requirements for the project. The General Staff then handed responsibility over to the Army's Ordnance Technical Committee. A sub-committee was formed and began work on the project on June 19 1940, beginning with a meeting at the Bantam factory. The committee wanted to discuss the project with the management and also assess the capacity of the plant.

Major (he was to be promoted Colonel) Howie left the "Belly Flopper" project to join the committee. Engineers from the Spicer transmission company were brought in to advise on the 4x4 drive. Three Army engineers, Bob Brown, Bill Burgan and William Beasley, from the Ordnance Department advised the committee and manufacturers on the basic requirements for the vehicle.

They stated that it should be four-wheel drive, have a crew of three, be armed with a .3in Browning on a pintle mount and have a ground clearance of 165mm. A rough sketch drawn by William Beasley indicated features

LEFT: A Ford built jeep modified by men of the Royal Signals in the 49th Infantry Division. It has cable drums fitted to the front fender for fast telephone cable laying.

BELOW: The ''guts'' of a jeep. The hood opened to show the 54bhp, 4 cylinder L-head petrol driven internal combustion engine.

such as the degree of ground clearance front and rear and the position of the machine gun between the two front seats. These specifications were approved by the Ordnance Technical Committee with the added provisions of a maximum weight of 590kg and a payload of 272kg. The maximum permitted wheelbase and track were to be 2.032m and 1.194m respectively.

Meanwhile, in Europe, the Germans had launched their invasion of the Low Countries and France (May 10 1940). They had seized northern France as far as the Somme and pushed the British forces back to the Dunkirk perimeter. The US Army, as well as the White House, identified the possible spread of the war and pressure to expand and equip the US armed forces mounted.

Manufacturers were informed that, if they were intending to enter the competition to produce the vehicle, they should deliver their designs and 70 vehicles, including eight with four-wheel drive, within 75 days. The first prototype had to be delivered within 49 days and the balance of the batch within 28 days. The budget for the program was $175,000.

The Quarter Master Corps invited 135

manufacturers to submit proposals – only two replied. In part, many may have been deterred by the time limit, but also the suggested low weight of the vehicle may have proved a problem for conventional truck builders. The two contenders were American Bantam and Willys-Overland Motors Inc.

At Bantam, the company President Francis H Fenn sat down with his predecessor, Arthur Brandt, who had headed the company when it was known as the Austin Car Co. Brandt suggested that they should bring in Karl K Probst, an engineer whose experience Brandt knew would be invaluable. On July 17 1940 Fenn proposed to Probst that he should head the project. Probst refused but having thought the challenge over, he accepted the offer. He was under no illusions about just how tough the job would be within the time and financial constraints.

Probst was now working against the clock – he had to deliver his drawings to the US Army vehicle test center at Holabird by 0900 hours on Monday July 22. In less than five days, he had drawn up technical specifications for what was to become the jeep. Probst contacted Spicer at Toledo and they agreed to supply axles and gearboxes. Bob Lewis, a Spicer engineer, proposed that they use the axle developed for the Studebaker Champion. It would push the vehicle's weight well above that specified by the US Army Quarter Master, but Probst was confident that no other competing manufacturer would be able to keep the weight down.

Probst chose the Continental Y-4112 as the engine since it was readily available and he reckoned that at 48bhp and 3250rpm it had sufficient power. Harold Crist, the Works Director of Bantam, and Francis Fenn helped Probst to find other parts suitable for the lightweight vehicles besides those which the company was making.

By September 21, Probst, having completed the drawings and sourced the parts, traveled to Baltimore to show them to Charles Payne, the Bantam military sales director. Payne, who had sold the little Austin Roadsters to the Army, expressed concern when Probst told him that the weight of the proposed vehicle was 840kg, a total which exceeded the weight specified by the US Army by about 250kg. Payne also realized that the specification document had not been drafted according to the US Army requirements and so a secretary was summoned from home to make the corrections. They worked through the night retyping it and took advantage of the situation by inserting the weight specified by the army in the vehicle description.

On July 22 1940 the initial tenders were received by Major Herbert J Lawes at Camp Holabird. Bantam had delivered within the specified 75 days, but Willys, who had had problems obtaining axles from Spicer, requested an extension to 120 days. Ironically, Willys offered to produce a vehicle at a lower price than Bantam, but tough penalty clauses, which raised the price of the vehicle by $5 a day for every day after the 75, pushed the Willys price above that of Bantam.

Bantam won the order with a quotation of $171,185 and, though they were not officially notified until August 5, they were sufficiently confident that they would win that they had recruited staff, tooled up and hired four extra engineers before that date. Probst now had to deliver the first prototype by 1700 hours on September 23.

Under Roy S Evans, the Bantam team excelled themselves and the vehicle was ready by the 21st, which gave the company two days to give it a test drive of 240km. It was an indication of the confidence that Probst had

BELOW: The Bantam prototype of the jeep which was delivered on time to the US Army Quartermaster General in 1940. It was to be copied and adapted by Willys who won the main order because the US Army thought that Bantam did not have adequate mass production facilities for the anticipated huge orders.

in the little vehicle that, with the Bantam company director Harold Crist as passenger, he drove the prototype the 270km from the factory to Camp Holabird, arriving with half an hour to spare on the delivery deadline. The first Bantam had some of the features that would later be recognizable as those of the jeep: cutaway sides by the driver and passenger and the slab-sided rear, as well as a robust front bumper.

The tests at Holabird ran from September 27 to October 16. The vehicle was driven for 5500km, 5000km of which were cross-country or over special test tracks. Representatives from Willys and Ford were present at Holabird and followed the tests with considerable interest. In ordinary commercial practise, this access would have been very unusual but, when questioned about this, the Quarter Master explained that the Bantam vehicle was now government property and he was free to show it to whomever he chose.

The US Army knew that they might soon be demanding mass production of the new vehicle and suspected that Bantam lacked the resources to undertake this. Indeed, it was believed that it might be beyond the capability of Willys – only a giant like Ford could deliver the numbers on time.

At the close of the trials, there were some conflicting reports. While Captain E Moseley said that the Bantam prototype was the best ever tested at Holabird, others said the vehicle was too heavy and required frequent maintenance. However, any faults that developed, and there were 20 defects or breakdowns, were quickly resolved and the US Army report concluded: ''The vehicle had a good power output and met the requirements of the service.''

Bantam noted the comments and incorporated modifications in subsequent models. The Bantam Mark II had redesigned front fenders, which looked even closer to the classic jeep shape, and grab handles above the rear wheels. By December 17 1940 they had delivered the whole batch of 70 vehicles, including the eight with four-wheel drive. It was an indication of the pressure that the US defense industry and armed forces were then under that the decision was taken to order 1500 of these vehicles on that basis of the first test report.

Unfortunately, this order saw the beginning of a commercial controversy which would dog the development and production

ABOVE LEFT: A pre-production Bantam showing head light grills and early canvas tilt.

LEFT: A Bantam in service with the 6th Armoured Division of the British Army. It has a .303in Bren light machine gun on an AA mount fitted on the passenger's side.

ABOVE: A Bantam 40 BRC which has a number of the recognizable jeep features, including grab handles, angular front mud guards and folding tilt.

of the jeep. Senior US Army officers suggested that the order be split between Bantam, Ford and Willys; the motor transport sub-committee of the Quarter Master Corps agreed and recommended this be adopted on October 18.

Bantam were understandably angry and Charles Payne went as high as Henry Stimson, the Secretary of State for War, with his complaint. Stimson and the US General Staff agreed the order should go to Bantam, but a political battle had developed between manufacturers, each supported by their military backers.

Willys designed and built two prototypes at their own expense – one with four-wheel drive and pressed components was included in the order. By November 14, the Quarter Master won his battle and, at the suggestion of Lieutenant Colonel Henry S Aurand, who headed the 4x4 program (and with the approval of General Knudsen) it was decided that each competitor should be awarded an order for 1500 vehicles – as long as they met the official specifications.

Bantam was supported by Senator R Reynolds, an advocate of four-wheel drive. On November 11, the Willys two-wheel drive vehicle designed by Delmar J Ross, the Vice-President of Engineering, was delivered to

Camp Holabird, and 12 days later the Ford vehicle called the "Pygmy" was delivered. Bantam were understandably irritated to see that their two rivals had copied many of the features of their vehicle. Interestingly, however, each had individual strengths and defects – the Bantam vehicle had a lower fuel consumption; Ford's had better steering and was more comfortable, but lacked power.

The Ford Pygmy cost $925 and was powered with an engine from a Ferguson Dearborn agricultural tractor. The Willys Quad was more powerful and had a better performance over the test track. The Willys received high praise from Colonel C C Duell who wrote: "The Willys engine out-classed all others in power and produced a brilliant performance."

However, the Quad weighed 1099kg and this was clearly a problem even though the Quarter Master Corps had raised the weight limit to 980kg. Despite the weight problem, Willys received a firm order for 1500 Quads and began looking for ways to slim down their little Quad. They decided that the engine should remain unaltered, so adopted the lighter stamped radiator grill fitted to the Pygmy. The new vehicle was given the name Willys MA Command Reconnaissance. With the orders confirmed, the Quarter Master

BELOW: The Willys MA which, with the exception of the front radiator grill, is the definitive jeep.

BOTTOM: A Ford built jeep showing the spare wheel and towing eye, but without jerrican brackets. "Ford" can be seen stamped out of the metal at the rear of the vehicle.

RIGHT: A late series Willys MB during signals training in the United States in the summer of 1941.

Corps, in collaboration with the Infantry, Artillery, Cavalry and Armor Corps, drew up the definitive specification for the new lightweight vehicle. It was to have:

Maximum speed of at least 88.5km/h
Minimum speed of not over 5km/h
Fording depth of 45cm
Capable of being fitted with snow chains
Maximum weight of 953kg for the two-wheel drive and 987kg for the four-wheel drive
Payload of 363kg
Approach angle of 45 degrees
Departure angle of 35 degrees

In the final evaluation, Bantam, who had been first in the field, lost out to Willys, but Ford, with powerful backers, nearly won an order for 16,000 vehicles. The Office of Production Management (OPM) intervened, pointing out that, besides the obvious breach of the principles of the competition, the Willys vehicle, at $739, was the best value. And so Willys received an order for 16,000 units.

Britain and the Soviet Union, which were now both locked in war with Nazi Germany and its allies, were beneficiaries of the early trials. Some 2675 Bantam 40 BRC, 3650 Ford GP and 1500 Willys jeeps were passed to the

UK and USSR as part of the Lend-Lease program. The 40 BRC was used by the British in North Africa and, because of its light weight was adopted by airborne units. The unit cost of a Bantam was just over $1166.

In the United States, refining work on the Willys included installing a new air filter which conformed with the US Bureau of Standards requirements and a 6-volt 40A generator was fitted to conform with those on other US military vehicles. Fuel capacity was increased from 37.9 liters to 56.8 liters. A Type 2H 6-volt battery replaced the civilian type fitted to the first series of vehicles. The emergency brake was moved from the left to the center. The tilt was fitted with a double hoop which gave passengers more space underneath. Brackets for an ax and spade were fitted to the left side of the vehicle, and black-out lamps were fitted. Other modifications included a mount for an 18.9-liter fuel can at the rear.

Under the designation Willys MB, some 361,349 were built. Demand rocketed as the US armed forces expanded and, on November 10 1941, Ford were awarded a $14.6 million contract to supply 15,000 vehicles. By the end of the war, Ford had built 277,896 GPWs (General Purpose Willys). However, the jeep was to see a lot of action before that date.

The origins of a famous name

The origins of the name that is now common currency throughout the world and is used to describe any small 4x4 vehicle are unclear. According to a contemporary account published in Britain, the initials GP painted on vehicles under trial were seen by an anonymous GI who coined the name "jeep."

The Willys test-driver Irving Hausmann said that he emphasized the name to distinguish the Willys vehicle from the Ford vehicle which had also been delivered to Camp Holabird. The US press first used it in February 1941. American Motors registered the name as a trademark, but it has passed into common usage.

Before its universal acceptance, manufacturers and the media came up with names like "Bug," "Blitz Buggy," "Peep," "Midget" and "Quad." In British and Canadian use, the formal title for the Jeep was Car, 5-cwt, 4x4. One British writer in 1943 asserted that the GPA, the amphibious version of the jeep, was called the "Quack," while winterized jeeps were called "Penguins" — both names seem to have been a product of his fertile imagination.

The word jeep may be derived from the quaint fantasy animal "Eugene the Jeep" created by the US artist Segar, which accompanied the cartoon character Popeye. It looked a little like a dog, came from Africa and enjoyed a diet of orchids. Other sources assert that jeep was US Army slang from World War I and could be applied to anything that was out of the ordinary, odd or new.

If Popeye was responsible for the origin of the name, the vehicle enjoyed considerable popularity with cartoonists. Jon's "Two Types," two British Eighth Army captains, traveled through North Africa and into Italy, their jeep laden with bedrolls and brew kits. Its front bumper had the slogan "D-day Dodgers," while the hood had a cryptic comment in Arabic.

Bill Mauldin's cartoon of the cavalryman about to shoot his jeep as one might put a crippled horse out of its agony is well known. Others show his two dog-face soldiers, Willy and Joe, under heavy machine-gun fire in a jeep which has taken hits on the rear tire. The caption reads "I hate to run on a flat. It tears hell outta th'tires."

Army artillery forward observers in Tunisia in 1943 correct fire over a radio fitted to a jeep.

LEFT: US gunners in a heavily laden jeep. It has AmeriCans – US manufactured fuel containers – strapped to the rear as well as the passenger's side.

BELOW: A jeep in Tunisia towing an improvised cable trailer. Packs and entrenching tools are slung from the vehicle.

According to US Army manual TM-9-2800 produced in September 1943, the standard jeep had an empty weight of 1111.2kg, a payload of 362.8kg, and a crew of two, with seating for four. Tires were four single 600x16 six-ply plus a spare wheel. Fuel capacity was 15 US gallons of 70-octane gasoline, which gave a range of 480km. The vehicle was 3.33m long, 1.57m wide and 1.83m high (or 1.32m with the windshield folded). The wheelbase was 2.03m and ground clearance 22.2cm. The engine was a Willys MB 4-cylinder in-line, or Ford GPW with governor, to give 3820rpm and a top speed of 104km/h.

While serving in the British Army's 51st (Scottish) Division, Robert Woollcombe had an opportunity to see the speed at which a jeep could be driven. While attached briefly to a US Army unit, he observed: ''There was constant movement between their positions, in full view of the canal, all day long. And whenever they moved for something, they flew about in jeeps – which they called 'Peeps.' These Peeps shot about on the slightest pretext – and the idea was that safety lay in speed. I got a lift in one. We tore up the narrow lateral road alongside the canal between the two outposts, with the land as open as a billiard table. The driver was the cheeriest of souls; 'Don't you get shot up?' I asked. 'Waal,' he guessed he just kept his foot down.''

The jeep had a conventional ladder-type chassis made by Midland Steel. Willys and Ford differ in small details. The central plate that was the anchor point for the machine-gun pintle was rounded on the Willys and rectangular on the Ford. Willys have an extra cross member at the rear. The shock absorbers were L-shaped on the Willys and bell-shaped on the Ford.

Suspension was based on leaf springs both front and rear. Though the jeep was a very rugged vehicle, drivers could wreck the sus-

ABOVE: US troops cook rations on a petrol stove in North Africa. Their jeep has a .3in Browning on the pedestal mount. The vehicle has the usual collection of bed rolls, axe and shovel.

pension if they took it at speed across rough ground. Some engineer units had a thriving business making sheath knives out of broken leaf springs which were hammered flat and given an edge. There were nine leaves on the rear wheels and eight on the front right, with an extra half spring on the left to compensate for the off-center engine. The hydraulic telescopic dampers were reinforced at the rear.

The brakes built by Bendix were hydraulic and consisted of drums on all four wheels. The handbrake was modified in the light of experience, and on later models with a transfer gearbox, the brake band was replaced with a drum brake. Many vehicles were modified after the war, and the French built Hotchkiss jeeps had a drum brake as a standard feature; Ford was credited with this modification, but it was also fitted to Willys vehicles.

The jeep was powered by a Willys Type 441 or 442 "Go Devil" four-cylinder in-line water-cooled engine with side valves, which ran on regular 70-octane gasoline and developed 60bhp at 4000rpm. Swept volume was 2199cc (70.375 x 111.125mm). The camshaft was chain-driven except on the last series of vehicles which had a gear drive. The compression ratio was 6.48:1; the spark plugs were either Auto-Lite AN 7 or Champion QM 2; the distributor was an Auto-Lite; and there was a special distributor sealed against dust. The mechanical fuel pump in the jeep was an AC model AF and the carburetor was a Carter Model WO 5395.

TM21-305, the War Department driver's manual, emphasized that drivers should check the carburetor air-cleaner when vehicles were operating in deserts, sand or dust. "If the outside air is full of dust and sand, the

BELOW: French troops in US supplied jeeps enter Tunis in 1943. They are members of the Army of North Africa and so still wear French uniforms, but by the close of the war the French were almost completely kitted out with US weapons, vehicles and even uniforms.

ABOVE: A high ranking Chinese officer inspects Chinese troops operating in the China-Burma-India theatre. The jeeps are supplied by the Americans, while the helmets and uniforms of the mule troops are of British origin.

air cleaner will soon become overburdened and dirt may enter and damage your rings, pistons, cylinders and valves.''

Transmission was a model 11123 Borg and Beck single dry plate, and the Model T 34J Warner gearbox had three forward and one reverse gear. The transfer box bolted directly to the gearbox was made by Brown-Lipe or Spicer and gave the driver the choice of high ratio in direct drive or low ratio with a reduction of 1.97:1. For four-wheel drive the driver engaged a separate lever. The low transfer gear range could only be used after engaging front-wheel drive.

The front and rear differentials and axles were made by Spicer, while the front axle constant speed joints were made by Bendix, Weiss, Rzeppa, Spicer or Tracta. As jeeps were sent to the Soviet Union and China, plates showing the gear shift were produced in Cyrillic and Mandarin script. In addition, a Spanish language plate was also produced.

The jeep had six-volt electrical equipment with negative earth. Headlamps were of the sealed-beam white light type. Auto-Lite built the dynamo, starter and voltage regulator. Jeep lights and batteries had other uses: at Anzio, Bill Maudlin observed that some dugouts were almost luxurious. ''Some blossomed out with reading lamps made from salvaged jeep headlights and batteries, and a few huts had wooden floors and real rugs and charcoal stoves made from German gas-cans and the flexible tubing that had been used to waterproof vehicles for the landing.''

A common field modification was to remove the near-side headlamp – this produced a modest weight saving, but also meant that the vehicle was harder to spot at night and could be confused with a motorcycle by enemy observers.

Before starting a vehicle the driver's manual *TM21-305* listed 25 preventative maintenance checks which the driver should

LEFT: US troops in a jeep approach Mont St Michel in Brittany in 1944 after the town had been evacuated by the Germans. The jeep has a tow rope attached to the rear fender.

RIGHT: Ox power takes over from horse power as Italian partisans use a team to tow a broken down vehicle in December 1944. Jeeps were parachuted to partisan controlled areas to assist British and US troops working with the partisans.

BELOW: Rain and muddy roads could even defeat a jeep. Here GIs of the 5th Army push a bogged vehicle and trailer on a track in the Gabbiano area in Italy in October 1944.

carry out. He was to check: 1 Tampering and damage; 2 Fire extinguishers; 3 Fuel, oil and water; 4 Accessories and drives; 5 Air brake tanks (on large trucks); 6 Leaks; 7 Engine warm-up; 8 Choke or primer; 9 Instruments; 10 Horn and windshield wipers; 11 Glass and rear view mirrors; 12 Lamps and reflectors; 13 Wheel and flange nuts; 14 Tires and/or tracks; 15 Springs and suspensions; 16 Steering linkage; 17 Fenders and bumpers; 18 Towing connections; 19 Body, load and tarpaulin; 20 Decontaminator; 21 Tools and equipment; 22 Engine operation; 23 Driver's permit and Form 26; 24 Amphibian services; 25 During-operation check. As the manual explains, many of these checks could be covered at a glance and a jeep or truck diver who followed them could have ''the satisfaction of feeling confident that your vehicle remains in the same good condition in which you placed it.''

The spare wheel was mounted on the right rear of the vehicle with a bracket for a spare fuel container on the left. This container was commonly called the jerrycan after the excellent pressed steel model manufactured in

Germany. The US Army entered the war with a screw-topped container which was dubbed the "American"; it was a marked improvement over British fuel cans which were known as "flimsies."

Photographs of British SAS Jeeps in North Africa (1941-43) show them loaded with a mixture of both German and US cans, but by 1944 the Allies had adopted the jerrycan. Martin Wolfe in his book *Green Light*, a history of the USAAF's 81st Troop Carrier Group, writes: "We learned how to run cords through the handles of those wonderful jerrycans and tie them down securely to the plane's floor rings. They could be lifted and stacked easily. They were filled with diesel fuel or gasoline, depending on which kinds of tanks or trucks needed them."

A towrope was often wrapped around the front bumper and a two-meter angled iron picket with a notch at the top was also welded to the bumper to cut or deflect wire or telephone lines that were often stretched across the road. Without this addition, low-slung wires could inflict ghastly injuries on the crews of jeeps who had lowered the windshield and were moving at speed.

Tools carried included axes, shovels and pick-axes; these could be used by the crew to dig-in if there was an air or artillery threat or to recover a bogged vehicle. Other common modifications included bolting ammunition boxes to the front fenders for secure stowage.

In *Up Front*, cartoonist Bill Mauldin pays tribute to "Jeanie" his jeep. "Two hundred miles is a long way for a jeep, even such a jeep as my pampered and well-manicured 'Jeanie' who had covered more than 16,000km of Anzio, Italy, and France. The ordnance people called her the most neurotic jeep in Europe. But they cleaned out the carbon, ground valves, and adjusted the carburetor. In spite of all this tender care, 'Jeanie' developed ignition trouble on the way north and I had to stop every few kilometers in pouring rain and get out and get under. After the first 160 kilometers I was very glad the mud had

obliterated the name 'Jeanie' on the jeep's sides because I was swearing at the car in a way that would have crisped her namesake's lovely ears."

The payload of the jeep could be doubled by loading stores into the trailer which was designed by Bantam. It was suggested that Bantam received the contract for the trailer as a consolation for the loss of the original huge and lucrative jeep contract. The company designed and built 100,000 units.

The Bantam Willys trailer had a cross-country carrying capacity of 226kg which doubled on roads, yet its ribbed steel panels gave it sufficient buoyancy to allow it to float. It was 2.794m long, 1.422m wide and 1.016m high. Trailers were modified during the war and fitted with a hinged rear tailgate to assist loading.

The working weight of the trailer was often exceeded by soldiers in the field and one

RIGHT: Men of Popski's Private Army, an Allied Special Forces unit, move down a track in Italy. The jeeps are armed with medium and heavy machine guns.

BELOW RIGHT: Gunning the engine to avoid flooding, a US soldier exits from a landing craft during the liberation of Hollandia in New Guinea.

BELOW: The tilt has been erected on this US Army jeep as it drives past Mt Vesuvius to protect the crew from ash.

photograph shows a trailer crammed with 10 German PoWs, who were captured in the fighting in the Ardennes in 1944-45. At Remagen Bridge in 1945, a jeep and trailer combination was also photographed with 10 GIs and their weapons and equipment loaded on board. A postwar trailer, the M 100, was produced which had a hinged tailgate and, though slightly shorter than the Bantam Willys unit, it did not float.

In the amphibious landings in North Africa, Sicily, Italy and France (1942-44), not to mention the punishing island-hopping campaigns in the Pacific, the jeep was often the first soft-skinned vehicle to come ashore and, under these conditions, the buoyant trailer must have been welcome. In order to make the transition from ship to shore safely, the jeep had to be prepared for deep water. The preparations took some time and were only effective for eight minutes of submersion in

1.4m of water. Unprepared, a jeep could wade to a depth of 50cm. After the war, manufacturers produced vehicles with sealed engines and protected electrical circuits to improve the original's wading capabilities.

In World War II, however, a vehicle crew had first to protect the electrical system to prevent short circuits, ensure a supply of air to the engine for the correct fuel and air mix, vent the exhaust above the water level to prevent ingress of water, and lubricate all the components that were vulnerable to water, notably the engine, gearbox and axles. Seawater is more corrosive than fresh and so this level of protection was essential. The driver and his mate first cleaned all of the electrical circuits and then painted them with a red synthetic paint called Glyptal which had high insulation properties. This was in turn coated with an asbestos-grease mix.

The exhaust was trunked directly from the manifold through a flexible metal pipe and attached to the right upright frame of the windshield. A similar pipe made from reinforced rubber, attached to the carburetor in place of the air filter and running under the hood, was also clipped to the right upright of the windshield. It had a protective dome at the top to prevent the ingress of water. Slim rubber pipes were connected to the distributor and fuel tank to ensure ventilation.

The crew then had to use the asbestos-grease to coat the electrical system, battery, coil, voltage regulator, plugs, dynamo, starter, headlamps, horn, instrument panel, oil and fuel circuits, fillers and drain plugs for the gearboxes, and axles as well as the axle shaft. Finally, the crew coated the exhaust pipe with a fireproof paste, and an insulation compound had to be sprayed over the whole engine compartment.

It is easy to see why waterproofing was not popular – it was a rather mucky, time-consuming process and, after the vehicle had

RIGHT: A US Marine Corps jeep bogged in the black volcanic sand of Iwo Jima in February 1945.

BELOW RIGHT: Leathernecks hug the sand on Iwo Jima as a jeep stands abandoned in the surf. Fighting for the island cost the Marines 5,391 killed and 17,400 wounded.

BELOW: A US Army Corporal tries a bit of deep wading during training at Fort Oglethorp, Georgia, USA in August 1942.

LEFT: A British Royal Air Force officer at the wheel of a jeep fording a swollen river near Caserta in Italy.

RIGHT: Major General John Millikin commanding the 3rd US Army Corps rides through the flooded streets of Pont-a-Mousson, France.

BELOW: Men of Clearing Company D, 105th Medical Battalion tow a jeep behind an assault boat during training in Fort Jackson in July 1942. The jeep has been partially wrapped in canvas to assist flotation.

Destruction

In a force which had vast amounts of mechanical transport, the US Army was well aware that spares could be cannibalized to repair wrecks and that captured jeeps would give the enemy additional mobility. The Afrika Korps made extensive use of captured Allied equipment in North Africa and, to German officers, a jeep was particularly prized. Consequently, the US Army had a chapter in the jeep technical manual dedicated to its destruction. All spares had to be destroyed to the point where they could not be repaired, and the vehicle hulk should be left in a position which would obstruct the enemy. Of course care should be taken not to injure friendly forces while the destruction was being carried out.

It was only in the Ardennes in 1944-45 that there was any danger of US vehicles being captured in significant quantities. Some destruction did take place, but not according to the manual. Few soldiers would want to destroy a vehicle which was a runner, but nevertheless broken down trucks and jeeps could be repaired by the enemy or stripped for spares.

Several options were available. The simplest way to wreck any vehicle was to drain the oil sump and radiator, and with the gears in neutral, run the engine until it overheated and seized. Grit and sand could also be added to the engine to increase the damage. However, the official approach was more systematic. Parts could be broken up using sledgehammers, axes, picks or levers. Sharp instruments like hatchets and knives could be used to gash and cut vital components. This was most effective on the tires, though the manual also advised that the tire should be deflated beforehand.

More drastic methods were also available, Fire was an obvious way to destroy a vehicle — the on-board fuel could be used, as well as kerosene, flamethrowers or incendiary grenades. Finally, parts could be stripped and buried or even thrown into deep water.

The formal methods of destruction were listed in order of effectiveness. The first required the crew to empty the extinguisher and puncture the fuel tanks. An axe, sledgehammer or other heavy tool was then used to smash the distributor, carburetor, air filter, generator, ignition coil, fuel pump, spark plugs, ignition equipment, instruments and controls. Ideally, the cylinder block, cylinder head, the crank case, the gearbox and axles should also be destroyed. Tires were to be slashed. Fuel and oil was then poured over the vehicle and ignited.

The second was quicker — the fire extinguisher was emptied and fuel tank punctured. Artillery, anti-tank weapons or grenades would then be used against the jeep concentrating on the engine, axles and wheels. If a good fire broke out the vehicle could be considered destroyed. The third method again required that the extinguisher be emptied and the fuel tank punctured. Two 2kg sticks of TNT or equivalent explosives and two meters of slow fuse for each charge should be placed on the clutch housing and as low as possible on the left side of the engine. The fuse burned for about 200 seconds and the danger area was 182m for troops under cover.

been used, it had to be stripped off and cleaned down. However, if during a landing under fire, a vehicle flooded and stalled in the bows of the landing craft, it not only put the crew at risk, but could also block the ramp and hazard the vessel and its entire crew.

Interestingly, operational experience in 1944 in France showed that a jeep could ford depths greater than 46cm without special preparation, as long as the driver kept the vehicle moving. A World War II photograph shows General John Millikin, commander of the US III Corps, driving through the flooded streets of a French village with water lapping around the headlamps of his unprotected jeep.

Soldiers are naturally inventive, and in the US Army during World War II and after, there were enough vehicle engineers and jeeps to ensure that novel hybrids were developed. A stretched jeep was developed by the US Coast Guard and adopted by the Army; the long wheelbase was stretched and could carry 10 men. The Coast Guard vehicle was fitted with sand tires for beach operations.

ABOVE: ''Alma'' a jeep fitted for radio and with a wire cutter welded to the front fender drives through the battered town of Periers, in France.

LEFT: GIs take cover by their vehicles after a German sniper has fired on them near St Lo in July 1944. The lack of web, equipment and weapons to hand suggest that this is a support unit.

The 4x4 Cargo (Willys MB modified) was 70cm longer than the standard vehicle and was produced by cannibalizing disabled vehicles. The canvas tilt was also extended with additional supporting frame.

Six-wheel drive jeeps were developed for the US Army Tank Destroyer Command. The Command was looking for a fast, low-profile vehicle which would allow crews to engage enemy tanks with their 37mm anti-tank guns. The initial experimental vehicle, designated T2, was based on a conventional four-wheel Bantam 40 BRC vehicle, while the T2E1 was a Bantam with less extensive modifications.

Interestingly, the British took the vehicle and mount, dispensed with the 37mm gun and replaced it with a .5in Browning machine gun, and used it very effectively for desert patrols. However, the problem with the anti-tank gun version was that the two-man crew was obliged to dismount before firing the weapon which was mounted above the rear axle. In order to carry more crew and a viable

BELOW: Front line soldiers in the difficult Bocage country of Normandy in 1944 rest while a .5in Browning armed jeep stands guard. It has an ammunition box fixed to the front fender.

ammunition load, six models of a six-wheel vehicle, known as the Carriage, Motor 37mm Gun T 14, were built in 1942. These were 5.76m long. The six-wheel vehicle was also armored. Known as the T 24 Scout Car, this vehicle had a dual-drive tandem rear bogie. However, the 37mm gun became obsolescent and the General Staff increasingly favored dedicated armored cars like the M6, M8 and M20.

Armored jeeps were both factory-built and modified in the field. The Smart Company, which before the war had built bank vehicles, produced an armored version, designated T25, with a protected engine and armored windshield and doors. The T 25 E1 had more armor, but like the E2 and E3, it was too heavy. One photograph showing field modifications consists of an armored jeep in the Ardennes in December 1944, which could carry six GIs and had plate covering the radiator grill and windshield.

When Japan pushed north into the Aleutian Islands in 1942 and threatened Alaska, the Canadians and Americans began working on an all-terrain vehicle which could cross deep snow to recover downed aircrew. Bombardier of Canada, who had experience with rubber-tracked over-snow vehicles, teamed with Willys to produce the T28 and then the improved T29 half-tracks.

It had two front wheels which could be replaced by skis, while at the rear were six wheels, four of which were not driven and

BELOW: Men of B Company, The Argyll and Sutherland Highlanders of Canada in action in St Lambert-sur-Dives, France in August 1944. A camouflaged German BMW motor cycle combination stands abandoned by the Canadian jeep.

were 40x12; the two rear-drive wheels were 4.75x19 and had cleats which meshed with the metal reinforced rubber track. Tracks and wheels gave a low overall ground pressure. It was nicknamed the "Penguin Jeep." After trials the Allis Chalmers Half-track M7 was adopted in preference to the jeep. However, the M7 used the engine, clutch, gearbox and differential steering from the jeep.

The canvas tilt on the standard jeep offered little protection to the crew against cold weather and rain. Though open sides allowed easy egress and access they also ensured that the vehicle earned the nickname "Pneumonia Wagon." The British, perhaps because of their experience with bad weather, produced side panels. The Humber

BELOW: In the grim winter of 1944-45, officers in a radio equipped jeep fitted with chains watch men of the 101st Airborne in Belgium. The exposed sides of jeeps earned them the nickname "Pneumonia Waggons."

Car Company made an all-weather tilt with clear panels on the canvas doors. In the field, soldiers used numerous materials for improvised protection.

A cartoon in Jon's "Two Types" (the two imaginary, but entirely convincing, British Eighth Army officers who served through North Africa and Italy) shows their modified Jeep. The side panels have been constructed from ration boxes and bear such messages as Soya Links, Corned Beef, and Meat and Veg.

In reality, some modifications were very imaginative. Men from the 644th Ordnance Company of the US Army salvaged plexiglass panels from a downed aircraft and built an entirely glazed "hard top." Many senior officers had extended mud guards fitted to

the front of their jeeps which allowed them to display rank stars and unit insignia.

Field modifications were also employed to construct jeep ambulances, but versions were also factory-built. The jeep was to casualty evacuation in World War II what the helicopter was to become in the Korean War: it allowed the wounded to be moved rapidly back to clearing stations and thence down to the field hospitals and advanced surgeries. With antibiotics and plasma on board, a jeep crew could stabilize a casualty as they moved him to the rear.

Bill Mauldin describes an incident at an aid station in Italy: "The little field phone rang. One of the guys in the aid station answered it. It was Charley company with a casualty. The medic took his blankets off the litter he had intended to sleep on, and he carried it out to the medical jeep, which sat in a revetment of sandbags at the side of the building. They were back in five minutes, because it was only a 1000 yards, and they used the jeep because the hill was steep and the machine was faster than men on foot with a litter."

The flat hood was invaluable as one or two

RIGHT: A Willys MB fitted with "Mud Floatation Adapters" and a wire cutter.

BELOW RIGHT: Armored jeeps of the US 82nd Airborne in Belgium in 1944.

BELOW: A training picture of a jeep modified for carrying casualties.

LEFT: A jeep ambulance in the Far East. A frame fitted above the driver takes two litters with walking wounded and local helpers. Chains have been fitted to assist mobility in muddy terrain.

BELOW: US Army medics load a man with a foot wound onto an improvised jeep ambulance in Normandy in 1944.

casualties on litters could be laid across it, with a third across the rear. However, with litters across the hood the vehicle was over two meters wide. Ideally, two litters could be fixed to the rear of the jeep which made it longer but easier to maneuver. This left space for a driver and medical orderly. It was the British who developed a protective cover for the ambulance. The tilt was fitted with an extension over the rear of the vehicle which allowed two men to be carried under cover.

The US Marine Corps who fought through the intense tropical rain of the Pacific further modified the jeep by fitting a vertical windshield and frame which could be covered with canvas and which would take three men. An equipment locker was welded to the external body by the driver's and passenger's seats. The British and US Armies had a similar three-litter configuration, but without the canvas protection.

Ernie Pyle the widely syndicated and respected US correspondent, who was to die during fighting on Okinawa, paid tribute to the Jeep: "I do not think we could continue the war without the jeep. It does everything. It goes everywhere. It's as faithful as a dog, as strong as a mule and as agile as a goat. All the time it carries loads twice as heavy as those it was designed for and it keeps going just the same. The jeep is a divine instrument of military locomotion."

LEFT: A jeep from a Royal Air Force squadron in the ruins at Cleve in Germany in 1945. It has spare jerricans on the front fender and lights have been reduced to a minimum. The RAF roundel is painted on the hood for identification.

Though the jeep was a vehicle designed for war, its compact size and speed made it attractive to any young man in uniform. Moreover, the ready availability of fuel in operational areas and the skewed values that war engenders, made the theft of vehicles a constant problem for military police.

In *Green Light!*, Joe Konecny, a Squadron Engineering Officer with the USAAF 81st Troop Carrier Squadron, recalls: "While the 81st was at Melun, I used the jeep that was assigned to Engineering, and that way got to Paris occasionally. On our return trip that night we stopped for a snack and drink at a cafe halfway between Paris and Melun. When we came out the damn jeep was gone! Only a few civilians were in sight and nobody knew anything. So we started walking about fifteen miles back to base. Later when we informed the MPs about the theft, we found out that the jeep had been taken for a joy-ride and banged up by an escapee from a nearby military mental hospital. It took about two weeks to get that jeep repaired and returned."

Criminality of a different form involving jeeps is recorded by Philip Warner in his book *The Special Air Service*: "An enterprising American soldier, serving overseas, posted home the parts of a jeep, planning to assemble it after his demobilization. However, the postal authorities found some of the latter consignments a little too bulky." These stories reflect the immense popularity enjoyed by the jeep.

The Allies received many of the jeeps built in the USA, and they were also enthusiastic about their performance. The Russians received over 20,000 vehicles and at the close of the war, there were unusual encounters in Germany where Soviet soldiers driving US Lend-Lease jeeps met US soldiers in similar vehicles.

The jeep concept was extended to larger vehicles in the US Army inventory. The ¾ and 1-ton 4x4 Command Reconnaissance or Dodge Weapons Carrier, introduced in 1942 and built in Canada as well as the United States, was known as the "Beep" – Beefed-up jeep.

LEFT: A jeep in Roetgen, Germany in 1945. The crew are armed with M1 Garand rifles and the vehicle has the usual litter of stores and equipment.

BELOW: Jeeps in a convoy of US Army trucks moving through the shattered town of St Lo, Normandy. Allied air superiority allowed conveys to travel freely in France.

RIGHT: An optimistic advertisement from the Saturday Evening Post showing jeeps in action in China.

BELOW: The yellow lead vehicle of a USAAF B-24 Liberator squadron prepares to guide a bomber across a taxi way.

RIGHT: The jeep in action in the Pacific, with the US Coast Guard, another advertiser's eye view.

CHAPTER THREE

FIGHTING WITH OUR FRIENDS

The Soviet victory on the Eastern Front was won at a huge cost in both life and equipment. Tanks and artillery were mass produced in factories that had been relocated beyond the Urals, and millions of men and women were conscripted into the armed forces. While Soviet guns and tanks were crude by Western standards, they were tough and very effective and set standards which have remained models for many modern designs.

Soviet trucks, however, were archaic and many were lost in the initial German victories of 1941-42. US-built Lend-Lease trucks, which included both the terrestrial and amphibious versions of the jeep, gave the Red Army the ability to move fuel, ammunition and supplies forward to back up the tanks and guns. In turn, this allowed them to launch and sustain deep thrusts into German-held territory.

The British motor vehicle industry was well-developed before the war and worked hard to supply troops in the Mediterranean, European and Far East theaters. However, many vehicles were lost at Dunkirk in 1940 and, between 1941 and 1943, to the German

Afrika Korps in North Africa and the Japanese in the Far East. The British produced a range of hard-top 4x2 saloons and some robust six-seater 4x2 and 4x4 utility vehicles which were similar in style to German and Italian designs. In 1943, they even produced an experimental 4x2 "British jeep."

However, since it lacked drive on the front wheels, it was dropped in favor of the existing 4x4 jeeps in service with the armed forces. Nuffield Mechanizations Ltd of Oxford took the Willys design and shortened it to produce the car, 5-cwt, 4x4 Airborne, which was a two-seater. The steering wheel could be removed when it was carried in gliders or troop transports, and, though it performed "brilliantly," it never went into production.

In the United States, experiments with lightweight jeeps produced vehicles which, though less heavy, were not as robust as the original vehicle. The requirement was to produce a vehicle with a ¼-ton payload but one light enough that it could be easily man-handled. The Crosley CT3 "Pup" had a Waukesha-Crosley HO-2-cylinder air-cooled 38cu.in. engine developing 13bhp. It had a governed speed of 72km/h. The seats were

PREVIOUS PAGES: US Army Air Force ground crew in their jeep are dwarfed by CG-4A Waco gliders and C-47 transports which are readied for Operation Dragoon/ Anvil, the invasion of Southern France.

RIGHT AND BELOW RIGHT: Front and rear views of a GAZ 67 B a Soviet 4x4 equivalent of the jeep. Built at the Zavod Ineni Molotov plant in the grim industrial town of Gorki, GAZ vehicles have been used by Soviet forces from the 1930s to the 1990s.

BELOW: US Army Ordnance engineers overhaul jeeps. One has its wheels fitted while the body is lowered onto the chassis of another.

mounted in tandem. Thirty-six were procured and tested, including six which were evaluated overseas. The Chevrolet vehicle had an Indian V-2-cylinder, air-cooled 45cu.in. engine developing 20.5bhp. Its steering gear was centrally mounted and it could take 60-degree gradients.

The Kaiser "Midget Jeep" had a Continental HO-4-cylinder, air-cooled 84cu.in. engine developing 30bhp. The Willys MB-L Special was powered by a 442 4-cylinder I-L-W-F 134-2cu.in., which developed 45bhp. These "stripped" jeeps were known as WACs – (Willys Air Cooled), which was also a pun on WAC (Women's Army Corps). As stripped vehicles, they also collected the nickname "Gypsy Rose Lee" after the famous American burlesque artiste.

The British and Australians were responsible for possibly the most intriguing development in the jeep's varied career. Both countries worked on projects to turn the jeep into an autogiro! The Australians called their vehicle the "Fleep" and fitted it with a three-bladed rotor and aerodynamic body. The project was canceled because the operational need to be able to place a vehicle accurately into a small landing zone on New Guinea

Willys 4×4 Jeep, Ardennes, 1944

WIRE-CUTTER

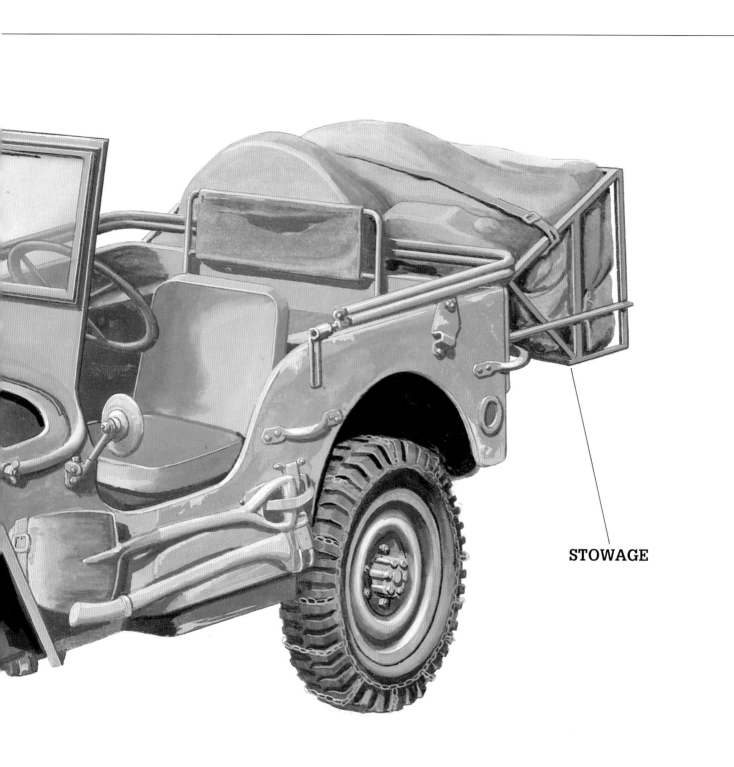

STOWAGE

SNOW CHAINS

ended with the recapture of the island.

In Britain, a vehicle named the "Rotabuggy" was built by ML Aviation Co., and was even tested. It was towed into the air at Sherburn-in-Elmet on November 16 1943 by a Whitley bomber. It proved difficult to fly and the tail was redesigned. The project was canceled as vehicle-carrying gliders were being produced cheaply and in quantity.

Photographs of the Australian and British craft show a very similar approach to the problem of making the box-like vehicle aerodynamic, though the teams were unable to exchange ideas, which might have made for a better design. The British Rotabuggy had a fully-enclosed cockpit and the rotor was faired into a camouflaged fuselage body with RAF markings. The nose of the Rotabuggy was still recognizable as a jeep, however. The Australian Fleep has a faired nose, but the rotor was supported by an open frame. Both craft had twin tailplanes.

Air delivery of the jeep by US CG-4A Waco or British Mk2 Horsa gliders allowed airborne troops to field a vehicle capable of carrying a gun or mortar crew with their ammunition. They were used during most major airborne operations in Europe and the Far East. At Arnhem in 1944, the six-pounder antitank gun and the 75mm howitzer M1A1 on Carriage M8 played a vital part in the defense of the British and Polish airborne perimeters.

In his book *Airborne Equipment*, the late Colonel John Weeks describes the jeep as "the saviour for the battlefield mobility of the Allied airborne forces." As he explains, the jeep did not make movement any faster, most paratroops still moved on foot, but they were able to take support weapons with them as well as radios and medical equipment thanks to the jeep. "Doctors found that they could pack enough surgical equipment into a jeep trailer to set up a tiny operating theatre in the field." The British fitted towing eyes to their

RIGHT: Towing 6 pounder anti-tank guns, jeeps of the British 1st Airborne Division move into Arnhem in 1944.

BELOW RIGHT: A jeep, with armour plate to protect the crew, is fitted with a double bank of six 4.5in rocket launchers.

BELOW: A Royal Artillery HQ assembles by its radio jeep at Arnhem in the opening hours of Operation Market Garden in 1944. The distinctive British Airborne trailer can be seen.

trailers so that a "train" of trailers could be pulled by a single jeep. While this was cumbersome, it did allow one vehicle to move a large quantity of stores over a short distance.

Britain also produced an expendable lightweight trailer for use with its airborne forces, with no suspension, motorcycle wheels, thin metal sides and a plywood base. Usually loaded with ammunition, they were designed to be towed off a landing zone to a rendezvous (RV) or gun line. To give some indication of the jeep's importance in airborne operations, British divisions had 904 jeeps and 935 trailers, as well as its lightweight motorcycles, handcarts, bicycles and other forms of man-powered transport.

The most dramatic development in the jeep's wartime career was its role as a reconnaissance and assault vehicle in operations in North Africa and Europe. The British Special Air Service Regiment has been credited with this innovation, but work had already begun

on arming the jeep in the United States. During 1941, a .5in Browning "Big 50" machine gun was jeep-mounted on a conventional tripod.

The experiment was not ideal and the Mount M31 was produced to take a .5in Browning on a pedestal sited between the two front seats. It is worth noting here that firing long bursts on a weapon as big as a .5in produces considerable recoil forces which require any mount to be securely fixed to the chassis. The M48 mount attached to the instrument panel in front of the passenger seat took a lighter .3in Browning.

Among the other experimental armament mounts tested were a twin .5in anti-aircraft fixture (by the Cavalry Board) in 1941. In 1942, US Navy Mk 21 and Mk 27 .3in caliber machine guns were evaluated as passenger-operated weapons. In 1944 jeeps were modified by the US Marine Corps and US Army to carry banks of M8 rockets. The configuration varied.

RIGHT: A restored Willys MB with tilt raised.

BELOW RIGHT: The rear window in the tilt was essential for the driver when he was reversing.

BELOW: US Marines fire salvos of 4.5in rockets on Iwo Jima.

In Alsace, France, during 1944 the US Seventh Army employed a jeep with an armored cab and a bank of 12 rockets in tubes. These could be fired by the driver and passenger from within the vehicle. The US Marine Corps had 28 M8A2 rockets in a T45 launcher, which consisted of two open frames attached to the rear of the vehicle. The crew had to take cover when the vehicle fired. The M8 had a 1.95kg warhead and a range of 4200m.

In 1944, the US Army evaluated a 110mm mortar mounted on a jeep. When it was fired, the weapon's base plate rested on the ground and the rear body panel of the vehicle had to be removed to accommodate the tube and bipod. By the close of the war, trials had taken place with T21 75mm and T19 105mm recoilless rifles (RCL). These antitank guns were mounted behind the front seats and were a pointer to the future of the jeep as an RCL armed mobile antitank vehicle in post-war operations.

In North Africa, David Stirling, founder of the SAS, was involved in modifying the basic Lend-Lease jeeps in order that they could

cope with the rigors of the long-range deep-penetration raids behind enemy lines. Three factors were crucial: fuel, water and fire-power. His SAS jeeps were fitted with a condenser for the radiator (to help cool the engine in the intense desert heat by recycling precious water), spare fuel in jerrycans attached to the hood and rear of the vehicle, and water containers strapped to the sides. An extra spare wheel was also fitted and the crews' large packs slung on the sides.

The SAS vehicles were armed with a .5in Browning and the .303in Vickers-Berthier GO – better known as the Vickers K – gun. This latter armament was taken from the obsolescent open-cockpit Hawker Hart aircraft. It was available in sufficient numbers in the Middle East for the SAS to equip some of their vehicles with up to five guns. It was a gas-operated weapon fitted with a 30-round box magazine and had a rate of fire of 650rpm.

Usually mounted in pairs, they could put down around 1200 rounds a minute, without the overheating problems of fast-firing single-barreled weapons. When the SAS deployed to Europe they retained this dated

armament, even though they could have equipped their jeeps with newer .303in Bren guns. The Browning used a 110-round disintegrating link belt which could be pre-loaded with a mix of ball, armor-piercing and tracer that was devastating against soft-skinned vehicles and aircraft on the ground.

By the time the SAS were in action in Italy and northwest Europe (1943-45), they were also equipped with mortars, .303in Vickers machine guns, and pack howitzers. They worked with local resistance groups and attacked German forces as they withdrew under Allied pressure. However, it was in North Africa (1941-43) that men like Stirling and "Paddy" Blair Mayne set the style for future SAS operations, including those launched into Iraq during Operation Desert Storm by Land Rover patrols.

By July 1942 the SAS consisted of 15 jeeps with 20 4x4 trucks for back-up. On the 7th, elements of the unit launched an attack on foot against Bagush airfield near the coast. Though most of their explosive charges detonated and destroyed enemy aircraft, some 20 malfunctioned, so to complete the work Mayne and Stirling decided to launch a jeep-borne assault. In five minutes, they destroyed 12 aircraft on the ground.

ABOVE: Major Ian Fenwick of the SAS at the wheel of his jeep in France shortly before he was killed in a Waffen-SS ambush at Chambon, France in 1944.

RIGHT: An SAS jeep in North Africa. It has a mixture of jerri- and Americans as well as camouflage nets and bed rolls.

ABOVE LEFT: Lt Col David Stirling on 18 January 1943 with a three vehicle SAS patrol commanded by Lt Edward McDonald.

LEFT: Lt McDonald at the wheel of an SAS jeep with its characteristic twin Vickers 'K' guns.

ABOVE: The British Land Rover Defender Special Operations Vehicle developed in the early 1990s follows the traditon of the armed SAS jeep.

At the close of the month, they hit Sidi Haneish, an important logistic base which had many Ju52 transport aircraft. The plan was for 18 jeeps to advance in line abreast and then, as they hit the airfield, adopt an arrowhead formation with each vehicle some two meters apart. Seven jeeps would fire outward and Stirling would be in the lead with two vehicles flanking him, and the navigating vehicle to the rear. Using the firepower of their Vickers machine guns they destroyed the aircraft in what could be described as a jeep-borne cavalry charge.

The war ended in North Africa in May 1943 and the SAS went on to conduct operations in Italy and France. One of the more remarkable jeep attacks took place on August 23 1944 when two vehicles under Captain Derrick Harrison approached the French village of Les Ormes. Unbeknown to the SAS patrol, the SS were conducting a reprisal operation against the village, burning the houses and preparing to shoot 20 of the male inhabitants.

An escaping woman villager warned the Anglo-French patrol and they were then faced with the dilemma of committing four men and two jeeps against a large, well armed force of Germans. They accepted the challenge. As they hit the village at speed, Harrison shot an SS officer and had time to see two staff cars and a truck. They concentrated their fire on those setting them alight. In a fast moving battle, the SAS killed and wounded 60 SS men and 18 villagers escaped.

By 1945 the SAS were deep inside German territory. Their jeeps had been modified and in Roy Bradford and Martin Dillon's *Rogue Warrior of the SAS*, Sergeant Bob Bennett recalled the jeeps: "The whole front of each jeep was covered in armor plate, with semicircles of bullet-proof glass to protect the driver and front gunner. Some vehicles were also fitted with a wire-cutting device above the front bumper. Armament consisted of twin Vickers for the front gunner, another

BELOW: Waffen-SS
infantry of
Kampfgruppe Hansen
pass a jeep of the 14th
Armored Cavalry
group abandoned
near the cross roads
at Poteau in the
Ardennes in
December 1944.

pair for the rear gunner and every third or fourth jeep carried a .5 Browning heavy machine gun. The driver had a Bren gun.''

Captured jeeps were also used by the German armed forces. In 1944, German soldiers disguised as GIs penetrated American lines in the Ardennes; they were part of Panzer Brigade 150 commanded by Otto Skorzeny which was meant to consist of American-armed and equipped, and English-speaking German soldiers. However, the search for this combination proved difficult – the plan called for 3300 men, 15 Sherman tanks, 32 armored cars, 198 trucks and 147 jeeps.

In the end, Skorzeny had to make do with under 1000 men, two armored cars, 15 trucks and 57 jeeps, though German vehicles were modified to look like US AFVs. Only 10 men could speak North American English and understand American slang, and a further 35 could speak ''King's'' English. These men were incorporated into a 150-strong force which comprised nine four-man *Einheit Steilau* units mounted in jeeps. They had three basic missions: demolition squads of five to six men were to sabotage bridges and US supply dumps; reconnaissance parties of three to four men were to reconnoiter the Meuse crossings and report on Allied troop movements in rear areas; and lead commando teams in three to four man groups were to proceed directly in the path of the German advance to issue false orders, prevent bridge demolition, create fake minefield markings to slow the enemy response, switch road signs, and cut telephone lines.

Lack of jeeps obliged the Germans to pack four men into each vehicle. This was a crucial error; by now, the jeep was in such widespread use in the US Army that its normal crew was only one or two men. The three or four-man German jeeps were obvious to US soldiers manning checkpoints in the rear areas. Despite this, eight jeeps did penetrate US lines on the night of December 16 and began moving freely behind the front. One

RIGHT: Military Police
check the identity of
the crew of a jeep in
Sedan in France in
December 1944, this
is following the scare
created by disguised
German infiltration
teams riding in jeeps
in the Ardennes.

team even reached the Meuse on the 17th, but the reputation of the force far outweighed its actual military effect, though one group did send the whole US 16th Infantry Regiment on the wrong road by switching road signs.

The German operation did, however, produce some confusion behind the Allied lines and GIs suspected anyone who was unfamiliar, even senior US Army officers. The confusion was compounded by American soldiers of German origin who spoke English with a heavy accent and came under suspicion. A number of the German commandos were captured and 18 were executed by the Americans as spies.

One man, Wilhelm Schmidt, told his captors that the mission of the force was to kill General Eisenhower, the Allied Supreme Commander, and this resulted in the general becoming a virtual prisoner for a time as security was tightened up. Only three jeep teams returned intact. Thus ended the only concerted use of jeeps by Axis forces in World War II.

LEFT: A liberator's view of Brussels in 1944. Waves, handshakes and flowers greet the crew of a vehicle.

BELOW LEFT: Lieutenant General Montgomery in a Willys MB during an exercise. The white flag indicates that the jeep is an umpire vehicle.

RIGHT: British vehicles including two jeeps in Vienna in 1945.

BELOW: US soldiers enter the grounds of a former German HQ, used by Hitler. The war is over and so their jeep is no longer loaded with weapons and equipment.

CHAPTER FOUR

VARIATIONS ON A THEME

One of the key military developments in World War II was the development of amphibious warfare. The jeep had a key role in many Allied landings. In the United States, Ford, GMC and Studebaker built amphibians which were used during the landings in Europe and the Pacific. The advantage of these vehicles was that they could transport stores and equipment from ships anchored offshore to depots inland in one lift.

When storms lashed the D-day beaches off Normandy in June 1944, the ships had to ride them out; the amphibious vehicles simply drove ashore and waited for the weather to improve. The shelving sandy beaches which would defeat conventional vessels were ideal for amphibious vehicles which could make the transition from sea to shore easily, or even cross rivers.

Many amphibious vehicles were built in World War II, notably the DUKW. The jeep itself was also modified to take part in such attacks. This vehicle was called the Truck 4x4 Amphibian (Ford GPA), better known as the "Amphibious Jeep." The first work on this type of vehicle was begun in 1940 by Robert W Hofheim of the Amphibian Car Corporation of Buffalo, New York, but he ran out of funds before his concept was completed.

About a year later, funds became available and P C Putnam of the National Defense Research Committee was given the task of developing an amphibious vehicle. He brought in Roderick Stephens Jr whose company, Sparkman and Stephens, designed hulls for racing yachts. Their collaboration produced the amphibious DUKW, and Marmom-Herrington, which called itself "the mechaniza-

PREVIOUS PAGE: Generals MacArthur, Sutherland and Krueger stand by MacArthur's GPA on Leyte in 1944.

BELOW: A jeep stops to allow "Merrill's Marauders" to pass in Burma in 1944.

RIGHT: General "Vinegar Joe" Stilwell rides a jeep in Burma holding his M1 carbine.

BELOW RIGHT: General Stilwell watches as his Indian driver services his jeep.

tion laboratory of the United States Army'', was given the job of developing the first amphibious jeep.

The company had already collaborated with Ford before the war and so they teamed up once again and together delivered the first vehicle on February 18 1942. The operational philosophy behind the GPA was that it would allow reconnaissance forces to by-pass demolished bridges and cross other water obstacles without any delay in the advance.

Two months later, the first contract was signed for the General Purpose Amphibian – GPA. Contract number 398-QM-12 937 was for 7896 vehicles and it was followed by W-374-ORD-2782 for 2104 GPAs. Jean-Gabriel Jeudy and Marc Tararine have identified an interesting discrepancy in the final production figures for the GPA. The US Army stated that 12,788 GPAs were built whereas Ford's figure was 12,785. To further compound the confusion, Bart Vanderveen quotes a total order figure 12,778 but says that ''only less than half this number were produced.'' However, production lasted from September 1942 to June 1943.

In practice, the GPA enjoyed only limited success with the British and US Armies. It was 606kg heavier than the jeep, had a modest payload of 360kg and space for a crew of two with seating for five. Critically, it had a small freeboard and so was fitted with a manually-operated bilge pump as well as one driven off the shaft. It could pump water out of the engine compartment, crew positions – or both – according to a valve setting. A wooden (later ribbed metal) splash plate in the bow could be lowered when the vehicle was about to enter the water. The GPA was made from sheet steel treated against corrosion, with cadmium-plated nuts and bolts.

The small size of the vehicle meant that part of its buoyancy was provided by the tires.

The GPA had an empty weight of 1660kg, an all-up weight of 2020kg, and tires were four single 600x16 six-ply with a spare wheel on the rear deck. The fuel tank held 57 liters of 70-octane gasoline. The electrical system was 12 volts screened and waterproofed, consisting of two six-volt batteries.

The GPA was 4.625m long, 1.625m wide, and the height to the windshield was 1.725m. The wheelbase was 2.150m. The jeep was driven by a Ford Type GPW (4 cylinders in line 2220cc, 60bhp). There was no voltage regulator on the first models. The gearbox had

ABOVE: Australian infantrymen cluster around a jeep on Port Moresby airfield in September 1943.

RIGHT: Marine Private First Class Harry Kizierian leans against a battered jeep on Okinawa in February 1945. The vehicle has chains on the tires and a .3in Browning mount for the passenger's seat.

three forward speeds and one reverse with a two speed transfer box. The maximum gradient for the GPA was 45 degrees, the angle of approach was 37.5 degrees and departure 37 degrees. The maximum range on land was 400km with a top speed 95km/h; on water the maximum range was 70km and the top speed 8.5km/h.

The engine was cooled by a radiator and forced air circulation which was drawn in through an intake in the front deck and exited through grill-covered vents level with the front seats. In water, air could be taken into the fan from two intakes in the driving compartment and exhausted from a grill behind the windshield. The driver used the steering wheel conventionally when afloat as it also operated the rudder at the stern via a system of cables and pulleys. The GPA also had a capstan and anchor which could be operated off the engine.

The GPA was almost the antithesis of the conventional jeep. It was mechanically complex and expensive and, though it could operate effectively on rivers and canals in western Europe, it could not climb the steep banks associated with many of these stretches of water. River crossings were therefore undertaken by the more robust and tracked Alligators and Buffalos, or conventional assault boats. In the USSR, however, it was a considerable success. Rivers in Russia were far wider than the Seine or Rhine and generally had shelving shores and sand bars, not unlike a beach.

On April 18 1945 Marshal Rokossovsky's 2nd Byelorussian Front of the Red Army was in position between Schwedt and Stettin and faced men of General Hasso von Manteuffel's Third Panzer Army who were holding a line based along the Eastern and Western Oder Rivers. Deliberate flooding had created a three-kilometer wide belt of marshland between the rivers. Contemporary film shows Soviet-crewed GPAs entering the river near Garz to assist in the punch through the center of the German defenses.

After the war, the USSR developed its own

RIGHT: General George S Patton crosses the river Seine on 26 August 1944 riding in his customized jeep.

BELOW RIGHT: US Army paratroops grouped around a jeep on an airfield on Luzon, Phillipines in June 1945.

BELOW: Two New Guinea islanders ride in the back of an Australian Army jeep to serve as guides during operations in April, 1944.

VIP Jeeps

The jeep was often the chosen mode of transport for almost all the Allied military and political leaders in World War II. In January 1943 President Roosevelt, while attending the Casablanca Conference, visited US troops in Morocco. During the trip he traveled in a standard jeep. At the Yalta Conference in February 1945, when his health was beginning to fail, he inspected a Soviet guard of honor from a specially modified Lend-Lease jeep.

Before the D-day landings, the British Royal Family paid visits to units in training. A photograph taken on May 21 1944 shows Queen Elizabeth, now the Queen Mother, visiting a Highland infantry regiment in a jeep. Though the vehicle was spotless and a smart corporal sat at the driving wheel, the crew have not expunged the flames painted on the bodywork above the silencer.

On June 4 General Mark Clark entered Rome and a photograph shows him in his jeep talking to a priest in St Peter's Square. The general's jeep has a wire-cutting angle iron on the fender and positioned on the left, a plate showing the three stars of a lieutenant general, on the right his Fifth Army insignia.

Six days after the D-day landings, Prime Minister Winston Churchill visited the beach-head. A photograph shows him tucked into the back of a jeep lighting a cigar while he talks with Field Marshal Montgomery. Two days later, on June 14, General Charles de Gaulle returned to France; he came ashore in a DUKW and then transferred to a jeep which bore the name "Alice" and the cross-sword insignia of the 21st Army Group. The flamboyant General George Patton had a jeep fitted with a large red-leather seat, doors, and two long brass horns on the hood.

An interesting photograph taken in Burma shows Lord Mountbatten, the Supreme Commander Allied Forces, being driven to an inspection. The jeep has miniature flags of the Allies on the hood, ammunition boxes bolted to the front mud guards, an unditching plank lashed to the side, and a condenser for the radiator attached to the front fender.

When General MacArthur returned to the Philippines, he may have waded ashore in front of the news cameras, but he toured the islands by jeep. A photograph taken on Leyte on October 20 1944 shows him in a jeep which has its deep wading inlet pipe still attached, but folded forward.

When Allied forces liberated Paris in 1944, the veteran British photographer Bert Hardy captured the exhilaration of the parade that followed. He lent his service dress cap to a pretty girl in a summer frock and, as she sat on the windshield of his jeep, he climbed on to a truck that was preceding it to get a picture. As he photographed her, she gave a radiant smile and saluted. Later in 1945, the same jeep had new passengers when Sergeant Hardy brought in three Waffen SS soldiers as PoWs, seated precariously on the vehicle's hood.

In 1945 General LeClerc arrived in French Indochina. His jeep was fitted with an armored windshield and, like his tank,

RIGHT: General MacArthur on Luzon in 1945. The jeep carbine clip cover can be seen in front of the wheel.

BELOW: A jeep hood serves as a table for the first meal eaten in Germany by Field Marshal Montgomery and Generals Simpson, Collins and Horn.

FAR RIGHT: Prince Bernhard of the Netherlands at the wheel of a jeep during a tour of liberated towns in Holland on his birthday.

BELOW RIGHT: Riding in a jeep which has been freshly repainted Prime Minister Winston Churchill visits Berlin in 1945, while Soviet soldiers look on.

bore the name of his family estate in France, Tailly. French and colonial forces subsequently became entangled in the First Indochinese War which effectively ended with their defeat by the Viet Minh at Dien Bien Phu in 1954. Jeeps had been landed at the fortified valley position and General Gilles took the wheel on a tour with Generals Navarre and Cogny after the successful airborne assault. Ironically, jeeps with inscriptions showing that they had been captured at Dien Bien Phu on May 7 1954 transported the Viet Minh members of the Armistice Commission at the close of the conflict in Indochina. The jeep had become a spoil of war with which to make a political statement.

versions of the GPA. The Soviet GAZ 46 MAV, built by the Molotov plant in the bleak industrial city of Gorky, was known as the "Malinki" or "little amphibian vehicle." Differences from the US original were few: the axles were not enclosed in the hull as they were in the GPA, and the propeller was not in a tunnel but protected by a curved steel guard. In the 1950s and 1960s, GPAs were used by emergency and fire services both in Europe and the USA, where they were invaluable for flood rescue before helicopters became more widely available.

In some theaters, though railroad tracks and rolling stock existed, locomotives had been sabotaged or destroyed in air attacks. Jeeps were modified in the field and fitted with railway wheels and operated in France, Burma and the Philippines. After the war

similar vehicles were used in French Indochina and Algeria. In Luzon, Philippines, the US Army ran a 30-kilometer jeep railroad between Bayagang and San Carlos using surviving rolling stock. The jeep conversion could haul loads up to 250 tonnes.

In Burma, jeeps and trailers operated on the railroad between Myitkyina and Baugang. A photograph taken in 1944 shows a British Royal Engineer squadron jeep converted to operate on the track between Cherbourg and Caen. The railroad wheels were attached to the outer rims of the standard wheels which have been stripped of their tires. The vehicle has two cans of lubricating oil attached to the front fender and a neatly rolled camouflage net which was stowed across the hood.

In Indochina, the French used railroad jeeps to patrol stretches of track that were vulnerable to ambush by the Viet Minh. They were equipped with an armored windshield and with a light machine gun fitted in the passenger position. In Algeria, in 1957, the armor protection was increased to protect the radiator grill and the crews. A light frame could be fitted with a canvas tilt.

LEFT: Sapper J Duffy and L/Cpl L H Townsend in a jeep modified to run on a section of the Cherbourg-Caen railroad.

BELOW: The jeep in service with the French armed forces in Algeria in the 1950s. The windshield has been hit three times by rounds fired by the FLN.

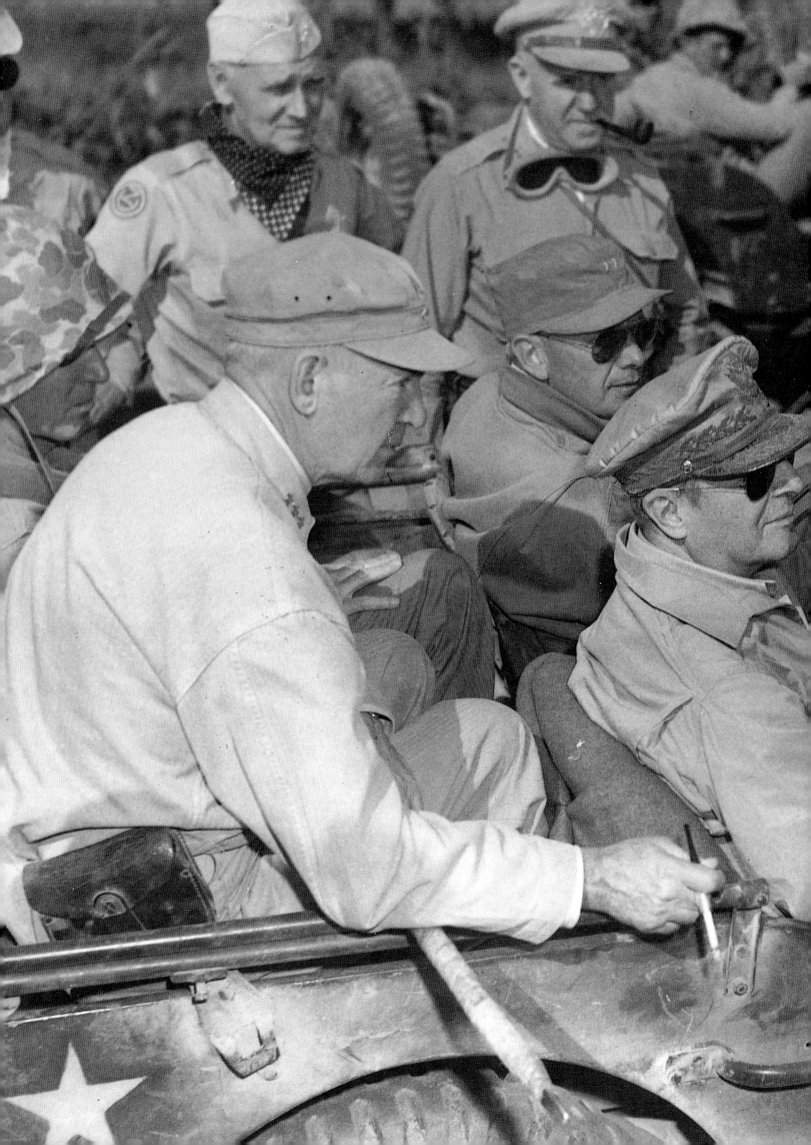

ABOVE: Exhausted Marines slump on and on in a jeep in December 1950 during the bitter Korean winter.

The vast numbers of jeeps that had been built during World War II ensured that the vehicle would remain in service well into the 1960s. Jeeps were widely used in Korea as ambulances, as telephone line layers, for Military Police patrols, and they were fitted with armored plate for reconnaissance patrols.

In *About Face*, Colonel David Hackworth, who as a young NCO in Korea received a battlefield commission, quotes from General Matthew Ridgway's biography: "I rode in an open jeep, and would permit no jeep with the top up to operate in the combat zone. Riding in a closed vehicle in a battle area puts a man in the wrong frame of mind. It gives him an

erroneous sense of warmth, of safety. His mental attitude is that of an ostrich poking his head in the sand. Also, I held to the old-fashioned idea that it helped the spirits of the men to see the 'Old Man' up there, in the snow and sleet and mud, sharing the same cold, miserable existence they had to endure. As a consequence, I damn near froze."

The French Army which was almost equipped from scratch with US Army weapons and vehicles before and after the war, made extensive use of jeeps in Indochina and Algeria. Jeeps were landed at the famous Dien Bien Phu base in northern Vietnam and, on March 13 1954, when the Viet

PREVIOUS PAGES:
General MacArthur,
C-in-C UN Forces in
Korea, in September
1950 at a US Marine
Corps command post.

BELOW: A jeep fitted
for radio stops by
men of the GHQ
Raider Co, Special
Attack Battalion, X
Corps near Yechon,
Korea.

ABOVE: US Military
Police with a young
North Korean PoW.
He rides the hood of
the jeep where his
captors can keep him
under observation.

Minh artillery opened up with the first of the barrages that would eventually pound the French into submission, they felt the full force of the bombardment.

"The whole French position looked, as so many observers had already stated, like a huge Boy Scout jamboree, with its tents, the rising smoke of the many cooking fires, and the laundry laid out to dry over the strands of barbed wire," wrote Bernard Fall in *Hell in a Very Small Place*. "For a few seconds the camera seemed to 'zoom' in on the flapping laundry and on a jeep racing like a little toy on the dusty road between Claudine and Huguette [codenames of French defensive positions]. And then this whole bucolic scene suddenly dissolved in what seemed to be a fantastic series of ferocious black tornadoes which completely covered the neat geometrical outlines of the French position."

The jeeps at Dien Bien Phu did not have

LEFT: French general Christian de Castries, Defense Minister Pleven and General Cogny on a tour of Dien Bien Phu in 1954.

RIGHT: Israeli troops with US jeeps and ex-Wehrmacht MG34 machine guns.

BELOW LEFT: An Israeli Willys jeep in 1948, with MG34s and carrying a litter.

BELOW: Arabs practise studied indifference to a jeep load of Israeli soldiers in the occupied town of El Majdal in 1948.

armored hoods and, with radiators hit by numerous shell fragments and small arms fire, many of them were soon off the road. Some veterans of the siege (and Hitler's armed forces) spoke favorably of the air-cooled engine of the Volkswagen Kubelwagen which would have kept running under these circumstances.

On November 6 1956 British and French paratroops landed at Gamil airfield, Port Fuad and Port Said to repossess the Suez Canal. The jeep went into action with the British paratroops, more by accident than design. By 1956, the Parachute Regiment was driving the Austin Champ; however, the heavy lift Handley Page Hastings transport could not accommodate the Champ and jeeps were substituted at the last minute.

Photographs taken at Gamil show men of the 3rd Parachute Battalion grouped around a sand-yellow jeep that had been landed not far from the control tower. In the Middle East, the jeep would continue in service with both Arab and Israeli armies, as well as UN forces policing the borders between the warring states.

Postwar developments in antitank weapons gave the jeep a new role as a mobile firing post for missiles or as a mount for recoilless antitank guns (RCLs). The US Army evaluated a 75mm RCL in a jeep, but experience of the tough armor of North Korean and Chinese T-34 tanks in Korea prompted a move to the 106mm M40 and its variants the M40A2 and M40A4. The M40 had a maximum effective range of 1100m and a good crew could fire one round a minute. The M40 could fire antipersonnel rounds which had a maximum range of 3300m.

The jeep-mounted gun allowed the crew to carry ammunition and use "shoot and scoot" tactics against enemy armor – a form of mobile ambush. The jeep and gun combination was adopted by many armies, including the Austrian, Brazilian, French, Spanish, Korean and Portuguese. The barrel of the RCL was 3404mm long and the jeep's windshield had to be redesigned with a slot in the middle to accommodate it in the traveling position.

Missiles extended the range and increased the punch for antitank jeeps. The French did some interesting pioneering work with the SS

ABOVE: An Israeli M38A1 drives through the eastern part of Kantara on the Suez Canal in July 1969. The tilt and doors have been fitted to protect the passengers against the dust.

ABOVE: An M38A1 heads up a convoy of vehicles and paratroopers moving along the Suez-Cairo road during the 1973 War. The vehicle is armed with an FN MAG machine gun and fitted for radio.

10 ENTAC wire-guided antitank missiles (ATGW) mounted on their M201 Hotchkiss jeep. The vehicle normally mounted four missiles in boxes bolted to its sides. A further enhancement came with the Milan ATGW. The firing post was fixed to a central pillar just behind the driver's and passenger's seats and reloads were attached to the rear of the vehicle where the spare wheel and jerrycan are normally carried. The spare wheel was fixed to the side of the jeep just behind the driver's seat. It was a tidy layout, and a Milan-armed jeep could hit targets up to 2500m away with a missile carrying a 2.98kg warhead.

Jeeps were also used to carry battlefield radars like the ZB298 device before more sophisticated systems like thermal imagery made active sensors like radar obsolescent. The jeep and its clones remain invaluable for artillery observers, and company or battalion headquarters in light infantry units. It can carry radios powerful enough to reach forward company positions and also to receive orders and pass information up to brigade headquarters. While the senior officer is out on foot with men carrying a short-range radio

set, the second-in-command is able to stay with the vehicle in order to relay or log any messages.

French jeeps were again in action on May 19 1978 when paratroopers jumped over Kolwezi in Zaire. The paratroopers had been sent on a mercy mission to rescue Europeans trapped in the mining town by rebellious Katangese. After landing and securing the town, they sent jeep patrols out into the bush. The vehicles were armed with the AA52 machine gun and the crew carried their personal weapons.

The French jeep is one of a variety of similar vehicles built around the world after the war. The license to organize and market spares for wartime jeeps, as well as the right to build the jeep, had been granted to Hotchkiss by Willys in 1952. In the 1950s, the French Army had conducted trials for a new cross-country vehicle, but had returned to the Hotchkiss M201 and, when production was finally halted in 1966, the company had built 27,604 for the French armed forces.

Builders of actual jeeps or jeep clones include the Japanese with the Truck, 4x4 Utility, or the Mitsubishi jeep L54A, which has a

RIGHT: A United Nations M38A1CDN – a Canadian-built version of the AM General M38A1 on patrol in Cyprus. The vehicle is in UN white finish with the Canadian maple leaf insignia on mudguard and sides. As the vehicle for the Commander Sector 4 it carries two radios. One to communicate with monitors and observers under command and the second to transmit and receive information with higher command. A second M38A1 CDN follows as a back-up vehicle and escort. The M38A1 is powered by a Willys 4-cylinder petrol engine developing 72bhp at 4000rpm. It has a top speed of 88.5km/h on the road and a range of 450 km. Though it has been replaced in front line service, it still finds buyers for its diesel-engined versions.

LEFT: Former President and General Dwight D Eisenhower rides in an M151 bearing his five-star insignia. He has just visited the US military cemetery at Saint laurent-Sur-Mer in Normandy.

BELOW: US soldiers in an M151 guard Cuban laborers captured on Grenada in 1983. The vehicle has a wire-cutter fitted and two M60 machine guns, as well as camp cots strapped to the hood and ALICE packs dumped in the rear.

four-cylinder, 2.2-liter petrol engine with 4F1R gearbox and two-speed transfer box. The wheelbase is 2020mm. Overall length and width is 3330x1595mm and the weight 1240kg. It is basically the US jeep CJ3B. The Truck 4x4 (Mitsubishi Jeep J24A), or Type 73 Small Truck, is another clone. It has a longer body than the CJ3B and is powered by a 4DR5 four-cylinder diesel engine developing 2659cc, 59kW/80bhp at 3500rpm.

The Republic of Korea and Brazil also manufacture versions of the jeep CJ5. The Korean vehicle differs from the US model in many details and is produced as the KM410 utility truck, KM411 ambulance, KM412 TOW and KM414 106mm RCL. It is powered by a Model MVA2000 four-cylinder, 1985cc (82x94mm), 52.2kW/70bhp, 4000rpm petrol

engine. The Truck 4x4 (Keohwa M-5 and M-7) resemble the CJ5. The Korean M-5GA2 mounts an RCL, while the M-7GA1 is the basic utility truck. The M-7GA3 has a machine gun, the M-7AG5 a searchlight, the M-7AG6 is an ambulance, and the M-7GA7 and 8 are TOW missile vehicles. They are powered by a 4229cc AMC six-cylinder petrol engine developing 85kW/114bhp at 3200rpm.

The Brazilian Truck 4x4 (Ford U-50 Campaign) is the outcome of the merger in 1969 of Willys Overland (Brasil) and Ford Motor (Brasil). The Campaign is a short wheelbase version of the CJ45 and is used as the mount for the 106mm RCL. It is powered by a four-cylinder 2300cc petrol engine developing 67.9kW/91bhp (gross) at 5000rpm. The spare

BELOW: A US Marine Corps M151 stops to allow a goatherd to pass during the Multi-National Force Deployment to Lebanon in 1983. The extension to the rear exhaust pipe on the left allows the vehicle to wade.

wheel on the RCL-armed vehicle is attached forward of the passenger's seat with the jerrycan mounted on a bracket behind him. This arrangement leaves the back of the U-50 clear for the crew to operate the recoilless rifle.

In Spain the US jeep CJ3B had been license produced by the VIASA division of MMC (later CAF of Zaragoza). VIASA merged with Motor Iberica and vehicles produced for the home market were named jeep Ebro and jeep Avia. There was a long wheelbase CJ6, which unlike the US CJ6 had CJ3B sheet metal. The military versions were CJ3m and CJ6m which were sometimes prefixed HU – Hurricane petrol engine, or PE – Perkins diesel engine. The diesel is a Perkins 4.108 four-cylinder, 1760cc (79.4x88.9mm), 45.5kW/61bhp (gross) at 4000rpm.

The Portuguese Truck 4x4 antitank gun (jeep CJ6/Bravia Commando Mk II) is a US jeep assembled by Bravia of Lisbon. It is powered either by a four-cylinder petrol (140C) or diesel (Perkins 4.154) engine. In India, Mahindra and Mahindra Ltd first assembled jeep kits in 1947 in conjunction with Willys Overland Corp. The CJ340 Army model closely resembles the wartime Willys. The company is now building utility vehicles with either diesel or petrol engines.

Automotive Industries Ltd of Nazareth, Israel, have produced the M-242 (4x4) 450kg Multi-Mission Vehicle (MMV) which is, in effect, a larger strengthened version of the M38A1. It is powered by an AMC 4.21 six-cylinder in-line engine developing 115bhp, and is fitted with a Donaldson two-stage air cleaner.

The South Africans produced a lightweight airborne vehicle called the 'Jakkal' (Jackal); by using glassfiber and other modern materials the weight is kept down to 950kg with a 180kg trailer. The Jakkal is powered by a four-cylinder petrol engine developing 63bhp at 5200rpm. From the front the layout of the vehicle radiator and headlights bear a close resemblance to the wartime Willys jeep – albeit on a slightly smaller scale.

LEFT: An Israeli soldier lounges against the wire-cutter on an M151 in south Lebanon. It is armed with two FN MAG machine guns and carries radios.

CHAPTER SIX

THE NEW PRETENDERS

In 1950, the US Continental Army Command placed a requirement with the Ordnance Corps for a new vehicle. Research and development began that year at the Ordnance Tank-Automotive Command. A year later, the Ford Motor Company was awarded a development contract for the new vehicle and the first prototypes were completed in 1952.

A further batch was completed in 1954 and given the designation XM151, and in 1956 two further vehicles, an all-steel vehicle (designated XM151E1) and the XM151E2 (an all-aluminum version), were built and tested. The XM151E1 was selected for production in 1959. Ford received the first contract and the initial batch of vehicles was completed at the Ford Highland Park Plant in 1960. The M151 became the M38 (4x4) vehicle in US Army service.

Later contracts were awarded to the AM General Corporation. The financial year 1978 request was for only 3880 vehicles at a cost of $29.1 million. It was then stated that the engine of the vehicle no longer met emission standards and that the procurement would be the last for several years. At one time the production line was running at 18,000 vehicles a year, but it has now ceased.

The vehicle entered service with the US Army, US Marines Corps and US Air Force. It was exported to Ecuador, Egypt, Gambia, Greece, Indonesia, Israel, South Korea, Netherlands, Peru, Philippines, Portugal, Saudi Arabia, Senegal, Somalia, Spain (marines only), Thailand, Venezuela, and Zaire. Variants include the M107 and M108 which are communications vehicles with radios installed to the rear of the vehicle. The

PREVIOUS PAGES: US Marines train in Lebanon, their M151 has extensions fitted for the exhaust and engine intake to allow it to land in deep water.

BELOW: GIs sweat out a Korean summer by a jeep armed with a .5in Browning HMG.

RIGHT: President Richard Nixon rides in an M151 during a visit to the 1st Infantry Division at Di An, South Vietnam.

BELOW: US Army M151A2s fitted with the Hughes TOW ATGW at Pleiku in 1972. Reloads are strapped to the left of the launcher and the spare wheel bolted to the side to give the TOW a 360 degree traverse.

passenger seat faces to the rear to allow the radio operator to use the equipment.

The M718 and M718A1 are ambulance versions with a crew of two, a driver and medical attendant. They can carry a litter and three seated casualties, or two litters and two seated casualties, or three litters. The M825 mounted the M40 106mm RCL, but this was replaced by the Hughes TOW ATGW. Kits were developed to convert the M825 to the M151A2 standard. Ironically, in mid-1987, 25 M151A2s were converted to M825 standard by TACOM to meet a requirement from Somalia.

The M151 is powered by an L-142 four-cylinder, liquid-cooled OHV petrol engine, developing 72bhp at 4000rpm. Most vehicles have a crew of four. Range on a 56-liter tank is 482km, though the M825 with a 59.81 liter tank can travel up to 483km. The vehicle has a manual gearbox with four forward and one reverse gear and a single-speed integral transmission.

The driver can select either 4x4 or 4x2 according to the going. Ground clearance is 0.26m on the M151 but drops down to 0.21m on the M825. Suspension is by coil springs on hydraulic shock absorbers. The M151 A1 and A2 are both 3.3m long, while the M718A1 and M825 are 3.6m long. Widths vary from 1.58m on the M151 to 3.6m on the M825.

The ambulance is the tallest of the variants at 1.9m, while the M151, A1 and A2 are just under at 1.8m. In US Army service the vehicle could be armed with a pintle-mounted 7.62mm M60 or a .5in Browning machine gun. In Israeli service during the 1980s they had two 7.62mm MAG machine guns.

Colonel David Hackworth was forceful in his comments about the M151 and an accident with a young draftee driver which took place in Germany: "On the way back down it became quite evident that my new driver was losing control of the vehicle. The old M38 jeep could negotiate cross-country driving; the latest and greatest M151 could not. The jeep

ABOVE LEFT: A USAF M151 armed with an M60 machine gun near the hulk of a Douglas C-47.

ABOVE RIGHT: An M151 gutted after a Viet Cong bomb attack on US Army quarters in Saigon.

RIGHT: US Marines firing a TOW anti-tank missile on a range in the United States. Mounting TOW on the M151 allowed anti-tank crews to "shoot and scoot," engage targets, and make a quick escape.

went into a slide, and driver turned his wheels, and as night follows day, the thing flipped over.

"When I recovered from that, I looked up on the hillside to see the new driver trapped underneath the overturned vehicle. Gas was pouring out of the jeep, and the big command radios were throwing sparks; it looked as if we were about to see a pretty spectacular bonfire. The driver's legs were pinned under the jeep. I picked up the back end of the thing and, with Robbie, slid the guy out.

"I looked at the boy and knew he was gone. He wore that ashen death look I'd seen too many times. I started up all the old battlefield stuff – 'You're going great, kid. You're going to make it.' – while I watched him check out of the net.

"By a miracle, an Army helicopter was in the vicinity and evacuated the driver to hospital in time to save his life, though the injuries left him crippled for many years."

Hackworth was scathing about the M151: "the bottom line of the incident was that it shouldn't have happened. All this boy's pain was due to a newfangled Army-issue piece of junk, which had everything and could do anything except get you from point A to point B in safety."

The M38 of which Colonel Hackworth spoke with such approval was developed by Willys from 1950 to meet an urgent US Army requirement for a light 4x4 vehicle to replace the large number of World War II vintage jeeps that were still in service. The M38 was basically a military version of the standard CJ-3A civilian vehicle with a deep fording kit, a 24V electrical system and a semi-floating rear axle, and was very similar to the wartime vehicle in appearance.

A quick way of distinguishing them apart was that the M38 had a single sheet windshield, while the wartime Willys had a split windshield. The M38 was in production from 1950 to 1952, when it was replaced by the M38A1. The M38A1 had a more powerful engine, slightly more rounded bodywork and mudguards which extended to forward of the front wheels.

The M38A1C mounted a 106mm M40 RCL, while the M170 was an ambulance version with a long wheelbase which allowed the vehicle to carry three casualties on litters or six seated. The M38 was built in Canada as the M38CDN and M38A1CDN. A civilian version of the M38A1 was produced as the CJ5 and, surprisingly, this was brought into military service as the M606A2 and M606A3. The

BELOW: During Operation "Bright Star," the US deployment to Egypt in the 1980s, two M60 armed M151s patrol the desert.

ABOVE: US Marines of the 24th Marine Amphibious Unit, (MAU) deploy from their M151 in an anti-ambush drill. The vehicle has a radio strapped to the spare wheel.

M38A1 is powered by a Willys four-cylinder petrol engine developing 72bhp at 4000rpm. It has a manual gearbox with four forward gears and one reverse. It can carry 544kg and tow 907kg on roads, and carry 363kg and tow 680kg cross-country.

In mid-1979 the US Army issued a draft specification for a 4x4 High Mobility Multi-purpose Wheeled Vehicle (HMMWV). The competition attracted designs and proto-types from the FMC Corporation (the XR311), AM General, General Dynamics (the XM998) and Teledyne Continental. All the vehicles had a low center of gravity and only the FMC design had the engine in the rear. The FMC has been described as a "trendsetter" since it was a private venture produced in 1969-70. The XR311 had a space frame and extra-large tires.

The General Dynamics vehicle grew out of the company's purchase of Chrysler's Defense Group for a reported sum of $348.5 million in 1982. Chrysler's expanded mobility vehicle project was taken over and variants were built with both Chrysler V8 petrol engines and North American Deutz diesel.

The original Chrysler vehicle had a rear-mounted engine, 3F1R automatic transmission, single-speed transfer box and full-time four-wheel drive. Eleven prototypes of the General Dynamics XM998 were delivered to the US Army in mid-1982 and evaluated.

The Teledyne vehicle grew out of the Mobility Technology International Cheetah developed in 1977 which had a rear-mounted engine. In 1979, Teledyne installed the 1HC 420cu.in. V8 diesel engine in the front. It was a sound design but remained nothing more than an experimental vehicle.

The LTV Missiles and Electronics Group of GM's General Division, the winner of the HMMWV competition, won an initial five-year contract for 54,973 vehicles worth $1.2 billion. Their prototype, completed in August 1980, was sent to the Nevada Test Center for extensive trials where it accumulated 21,000km of instrumental and dynamic test-ing by February 1981. LTV became one of three contenders awarded a US Army contract for the design and construction of 11 prototype HMMWVs (six weapons carriers and five utility) to be delivered in May 1982.

LEFT: Viet Minh troops with Soviet supplied trucks and captured jeeps move to take over Haiphong after the partitioning of Vietnam.

BELOW LEFT: A chow break on the hood of an M151 in West Germany during an annual NATO exercise period of the 1970s and 1980s.

BELOW: A heavily laden M151 heads up a convoy during an exercise.

In March 1983, LTV was awarded a $59.8 million contract by the US Army Tank-Automotive Command (TACOM) for 2334 HMMWVs which were then designated the M998 series. LTV named the vehicle the Hummer, however, this name did not take with the military customer who adopted the name Humvee.

Of the 54,973-vehicle contract, 39,000 were for the Army and the remainder were for US Marine Corps, Navy and Air Force. Production began at Mishawaka, Indiana, in early 1985. Contract options for a further 15,000 were exercised, to bring the total production by mid-1989 to about 66,000 vehicles

of which about 55,000 were for the US Army.

In August 1989, the US Army awarded LTV a further multi-year contract worth approximately $1 billion. The contract called for a further 33,000 vehicles until 1993. In service, the M998 Series HMMWVs replace some M151 jeeps, the M274 Mule, the M561/M792 Gama Goat and the M880 series, with 20 percent of the current fleet of M151s and many of the M880s being replaced by the Commercial Utility Cargo Vehicle (CUCV).

The Humvee has 2x2 seating on each side of the drive train which allows the front differential to be raised, together with geared hubs, to give a clearance of 0.41m, but it also

retains a low center of gravity. The windshield frame is robust enough to serve as a roll bar though soldiers of the 1st Cavalry, who had used M998s at the National Training Center (NTC) at Fort Irwin, told your author that it was almost impossible to roll a Humvee.

The production model of the HMMWV can be converted into different variants by changing the body configuration. The HMMWV is powered by a V8 6.2 diesel engine developing 150bhp at 3600rpm. The move to diesel is not only welcome for logistic reasons, but also because diesel has a higher flashpoint than petrol. The hood tilts forward and gives the driver easy access to the engine for maintenance. The transmission is automatic with three forward and one reverse gears. The transfer box is two-speed with full-time four-wheel drive. Steering is power-assisted which, combined with the automatic shift, makes the Humvee a very undemanding vehicle to drive over long distances.

The M1038 Cargo Troop Carrier fitted with a winch is 2.16m wide, 4.72m long, and 1.83m high, and it weighs in at 3493kg. It can lift a maximum load of 1077kg and tow a maximum of 1542kg. Angle of approach and departure are 47 degrees and 45 degrees. Maximum speed is 105km/h and the range on 94.6 liters is 482km. The HMMWV can ford 0.76m and, with some preparation, up to 1.52m. Spares commonality in the chassis, engine and transmission mean that parts holdings can be rationalized.

Over 3000 vehicles have been sold to 18 countries among which are Saudi Arabia, Abu Dhabi, Djibuti, Luxembourg, the Philippines and Thailand. The US Border Patrol operate civilian versions. The HMMWV proved itself during Operation Desert Storm and proved popular with its users – so popular, that the following signal was sent on February 5 1990:
Spoke with [name], 1 MEF Motor Transport Officer.

He understands there are not 35, but 159 Army Hummers missing.

RIGHT: An AM General HMMWV configured as a TOW missile vehicle. There are four variants of the ''Humvee'' TOW all with armor protection.

Star of stage and screen

Jeeps have featured in many films, they are a low-cost prop vehicle in which the star can make an entry, or which can be used to set a scene. In major epics like *The Longest Day* (1962) and *A Bridge Too Far* (1977), jeeps are an incidental in films with star casts and spectacular effects. In some films, however they enjoy what can almost be called a cameo roll. In *The Teahouse of the August Moon* produced in 1956, Glenn Ford played a US Army officer in Okinawa, who was seduced by the relaxed Oriental life style. In a memorable scene his jeep is coopted to carry a Japanese family of eight, with their belongings and goat — which nests comfortably on the hood.

Two years later, *Ashes and Diamonds*, the powerful film by the Polish producer Adrezj Wajda, opens with an ambush sprung by a resistance fighter given the task of assassinating a Communist official in 1945. The official in a jeep is caught in a hail of fire and the vehicle crashes.

In the opening scene of *M*A*S*H*, the film produced in 1969 which inspired the long running TV series, Donald Sutherland and Tom Skerrit travel to the Mobile Army Surgical Hospital in a stolen jeep. On arrival at the M*A*S*H, the colonel, informed that the jeep is stolen, calmly orders that the plates be changed. The film ends with the departure of our heroes, but not before the likeable, but ineffective padre has blessed the jeep and its passengers.

In *The Eagle has Landed*, produced in 1976, a jeep driven by a US soldier is hit by a burst of fire and as the windshield shatters it makes a spectacular crash into a mill pond. By the quirks of editing and cutting, the stuntman who crashed the jeep also played one of the two German paratroops who are seen firing the fatal burst — not many actors shoot themselves on screen!

Some 1700 have been at the Port of Jabel, with no apparent security. Army was advised by Marines, to put a guard on them lest some "walk off."

[Name] acknowledges that Marines may well have "borrowed" some of those vehicles; and, as a result, "10 were dropped off at a fuel point" and 1 MEF motor transport recovered an eleventh abandoned vehicle off the side of the road. [markings/plates were stripped; Army refused recovery].

He also understand the Brits may "have a couple."

RIGHT: A HMMWV with winch fitted to the front fender and with cargo space to the rear.

BELOW: A USMC "Humvee" cargo carrier with deep wading exhaust extension.

LEFT: In the Caribbean heat a US soldier in Grenada sits on an M151 near Greenville on October 25, 1983.

BELOW: An M151 of the 24th MAU in Beirut. The air intake for the engine can be seen on the right.

Bottom line: lax security and the vehicles were sought for parts. [Name] says the high-visibility of this issue has "nipped the problem"; he promised severe penalties for anyone caught with a stolen vehicle. The Marine Corps has filed MLSRs [military missing vehicle forms] on each one found in an effort to find the true owner [thought to be the US Army]. Kidding aside, any "borrowing" is looked upon as punishable and every effort is being made to return recovered Hummers to rightful owners.

When Desert Sword rolled into Iraq and Kuwait, HMMWVs followed the M1A1 Abrams tanks and Bradley armored fighting vehicles. One of the functions they fulfiled was communication through the US Army Mobile Subscriber Equipment (MSE) based on a series of shelters and trailers towed and carried by HMMWVs.

When the 101st Air Assault Division used 300 transport and assault helicopters to fly 2000 troops to set up a base 80km inside Iraq, they also lifted 50 HMMWVs. With the close of the war in the Gulf, AM General produced a stylish advertizement which showed a line of HMMWVs crossing rolling sand dunes in the red, dusty light of a desert dawn. In bold print across the picture they proudly announced "Riders of the Storm."

In the Europe of the 1950s and 1960s vehicle manufacturers looked at field cars and utility vehicles which could replace the jeeps that were coming to the end of their service with the armed forces. In Britain, competition to replace the Austin Champ was divided between the Austin Gipsy and Land Rover.

Both the Land Rover and Austin vehicles had the slab-sided shape associated with the jeep and both strove to emulate its robust simplicity. Land Rover won, and their vehicles, after being adopted by the British armed forces, have been widely used around the world. The air-portable 1/2 Land Rover which was first seen in public in 1968 could be stripped down for air-dropping, and in this basic form evoked memories of the Willys jeep. The latest vehicles in the Land Rover family are the 90 and 110 diesel-powered series.

In the Eastern Bloc, both China and the Soviet Union built the UAZ-469B and the BJ-212, soft-top utility vehicles, respectively. These were widely exported to friendly and client nations from the 1960s to the 1980s. The Volkswagen 183 Iltis (Polecat), a modernized version of the Auto Union Munga, was produced in West Germany for the Bundeswehr which received 8800 vehicles. It was built by Audi from 1978, and in 1982 production rights were sold to Bombardier of Canada, who now build it for the Canadian Army. Its replacement, the Mercedes-Benz 230G, was built under license in France by Peugeot with a Peugeot engine, and has been exported to over 16 countries.

Clones, copies and variants of the jeep design have proliferated in the decades since the end of World War II. Some of the modern designs are technically superior to the original, but they are following in the tracks of a little vehicle which from 1940 changed military operations and vehicle design philosophy for ever.

ABOVE: A French Puma helicopter with an M201 VLTT – the Hotchkiss jeep. The French-built vehicle had a few minor alterations like two radio antenna mountings and no wooden rests on the hood for the windshield when it was folded.

Index

Page numbers in *italics*
refer to illustrations.

Alfa Romeo 6C2500 car
13
Algeria 79, *79*, 82
AM General Corporation
23, 96, 109
M151 *1*, 8, *90-91, 94-5,
98-103*, 103, *108-9*
M151A2 *3*, 8, *97*
American Bantam Car
Co. 16, 17, 19-20, 21,
22, 32
Jeep prototype *19*,
19-20, *20*
Mark II 20, *20*
40BRC *21*, 22-3, 39
T2, T2E1 versions 39
*American Cavalry
Journal* 15
Amphibian Car
Corporation 70
amphibians *2*, 13, 23,
33-4, 39, 70, 71
Anzio 29
Ardennes 33, 40, *65*,
65-6
armored cars, M6, M8,
M20 40
Arnhem 53, *58-9*
Aurand, Lt Col Henry
21
Austin Car Co. 11, 19
Champ 86, 110
Gipsy 110
roadster 17, 19
Seven 11-12, 16
Auto-Lite equipment 28,
29

Beasley, William 17
Bendix Company 28, 29
Bennett, Sgt Bob (SAS)
64
Bernhard, Prince *77*
Bianchi S4, S6, S9 cars
13
BMW-built Austin
Seven 11
Bradford, Roy 64
Brandt, Arthur 19
British Army 12
1st Airborne Div. *59*
6th Armoured Div. *11,
20*
49th Infantry Div. *18*
51st (Scottish) Div. 27
Argyll and Sutherland
Highlanders *40*
Parachute Regiment 86
Royal Artillery *58*
Royal Signals *18*

SAS Regiment 15, 31,
59, 61-4, *62-3*
Brockbank, cartoon by
11
Brown, Bob, engineer 17
Brown-Lipe gearbox 29
Burgan, Bill, engineer 17
Burma *70-71*, 79

Chevrolet lightweight
jeep 54
China *29*, 49
Churchill, Winston 76,
77
Clark, General Mark 76
Cogny, General 77
Collins, General J.L. *76*
Commercial Utility
Cargo Vehicle
(CUCV) 103
Crist, Harold 19, 20
Crosley CT3 'Pup' 52, 54

DAF MC139 amphibian
13
de Castries, General C.
84
de Gaulle, General C. 76
Dien Bien Phu 77, 82,
84, 86
Dillon, Martin 64
Dodge weapons carrier
47
drivers' checks 28,
29-30
Duell, Colonel C.C. 21
Duffy, Sapper J. *78*
DUKW amphibian 70, 76

Eisenhower, General
D.W. *5*, 66, *90*
Elizabeth, Queen
Mother 76
Evans, Roy S. 19

Fall, Bernard 84
Fenn, Francis H. 19
Fenwick, Major Ian *63*
Fiat company 13
Balilla 13
Topolino 12
*Fighting Vehicles
Directory of World
War II* 13
Ford, Glenn 106
Ford Company 20-23
passim, 28, 96
amphibians 70, 71
GPA *69*, 70, 71-2, 74,
79
GPW *11*, 22, 23
Model T 11, 15
'Pygmy' prototype 21
U-50 Campaign truck
91, 93
XM151 96, 98

Ford Motor (Brasil) 91
France *17*, 33, *37-41*, 47,
48, 50-51, 62, *63*,
64, *70-76 75, 78*, 79
Frazer, Joseph W. 17
French forces *79*
in Algeria 79, *79*, 82
in Tunis *28*
vehicles of 12, 13, *17*,
82, 84, 86, 87
French Indochina 76-7,
79, 82, 84, 86

General Motors
Corporation 70, 101
LTV Missiles and
Electronic Group
see under Humvee
Gentil, Captain 11
German forces
on Eastern Front 74
in France 18, *65*
Luftwaffe *12*
in North Africa *12*, 37,
52
vehicles in 11-12, 13,
65-6
Gilles, General 77
gliders,
CG-4A Waco *4, 50-51,
54*, 58
CG-13A *54*
Mark 2 Horsa 58
Green Light (Wolfe) 31
Grenada 90, *108*
guns, anti-tank,
39mm 39, 40
75mm M1A1 58
six-pounder 58
see also recoilless rifles

Hackworth, Col David
82, 98, 100
Hamilton, Lieut H.G. 15
Hardy, Sgt Bert 76
Harrison, Capt Derrick
64
Hausmann, Irving 23
Herrington, Arthur W.
15, 16
Hofheim, Robert W. 70
Horn, General *76*
Hotchkiss jeeps 28, 87
M201 87, *110*
Howie, Col Robert G. 16,
17
Humber Car Company
41
Humvee (HMMWV) 101,
103-4, *104*, 109
AM General 101
FMC XR311 101
General Dynamics
XM998 101
LTV Group of GM
M998 8, *10*, 101,

103-4, 106, 109
Teledyne Continental
101

India, jeeps made in 93
Iraq campaign 8, 63,
104, 109
Israel,
jeeps made in 93
used in *84-7, 93*
Italian campaign *30-32*,
33, *36*, 42, 63
Iwo Jima *35, 60*

Japanese army 11-12, 13
Japanese-built jeeps, 87,
91
jeeps,
armored jeeps 40
British experimental
52, 58
definition 8
destruction procedure
37
evolution of 8, *9*, 11-12,
13, 15-16, 17, 18-19
featured in films 106
features of
brakes 13, 28, 30
carburetor 28
chassis 27
differential 29
dimensions 13, 27, 72
electrical equipment
29, 34, 72
engines 13, 19, 21, 30,
34, 52, 54, 91, 101
Continental Y-4112 19
Ford GPW 27, 72
L-head 54bhp *18*
for M151 98
Willys MB 27
Willys 441, 442 28
four-wheel drive 15,
17, 18, 20, 21, 29
front-wheel drive 15,
29
fuel capacity 27
fuel containers *26*,
30-31
gearbox 29, 34, 72,
74, 101
ground clearance 17,
18, 27
payload 22, 27, 32, 72,
101
radar carrying 87
rail modifications *78*,
79
range 27, 74
shock absorbers 17,
27
six-wheel vehicles
39-41
speed 17, 22, 27, 74
suspension 27-8, 30

tires 13, 15, 27, 30, 72
tools carried *27*, 32
transmission 13, 17,
19, 29
waterproofing 33-4,
37
weight 13, 17, 18, 19,
21, 22, 27, 72
wheelbase 13, 17, 18,
27, 37, 72
wire cutter *38, 43, 90*
operational
modifications 37,
39, 40-42, 45, 61-2
origins of name 23
prototypes *19-20*, 19-21
roles of,
for air delivery 58
ambulance, casualty
evacuation 42, *42,
44*, 45, 82, 98
communications 87,
88, 96, 109
machine gun
mounting *1, 10*, 11,
12, 15, *15*, 17, 18, *20,
27, 32*, 60, 62, *87,
90, 93*
missile carrying *10*,
60, 61, 86-7, *97,
99*
recce and assault
59-66, 82
towing 12, *14*, 58-9
for VIPs *5*, 76-7, *77,
90*
specification 17-18, 19,
22, 27
see also under
American Bantam
Car Co.; Ford;
Willys
Jeudy, Jean-Gabriel 71
Jon, cartoonist 23, 41

Kaiser 'Midget Jeep' 54
Kitzierian, Pte Harry *73*
Knudsen, General 21
Konecny, Joe 47
Korea *81-3*, 82, 91, *96*
Krueger, General *79*
Kurogane Type 95 car
13

Land Rover 110
1990 Defender vehicle
64
Lawes, Maj Herbert J.
19
LeClerc, General 76
Lend-Lease program
22-3, 47, 61
Les Ormes village,
France 64
Lewis, Bob, engineer 19
lightweight jeeps 52, 54

M38 *see under* Willys
M151 *see under* AM
    General
    Corporation
M274 Mule 103
M561/M792 Gama Goat
    103
M880 series 103
M998 *see* Humvee
M1038 Cargo Troop
    Carrier 104
MacArthur, General
    Douglas 69, 76, *77,*
    81
McDonald, Lieut
    Edward *62*
machine guns,
    .3in. Browning 16-17,
    27, 60
    .303 Bren LMG *20*, 63,
    65
    .5in Browning *1, 15,* 39,
    39, 60, 62, 63, 65
    M60 *10, 90*
    MG34 German *12*
    Vickers K .303in. 11, *15,*
    62, *62,* 64
Manteuffel, Gen Hasso
    von 74
Marmon, Walter C. 16
Marmon-Herrington Co.
    15, 70-71
    Ford LD1 4x4 16
Mauldin, Bill, cartoonist
    23, 29, 32, 42
Mayne, 'Paddy' Blair 63
Merrill's Marauders *70*
Middle East *12, 14-15,* 86
Midland Steel Company
    27
Millikin, Maj Gen John
    37, *37*
missiles, anti-aircraft
    Stinger *10*
missiles, anti-tank 86,
    99
    Hughes TOW *97*
    Milan 87
    SS 10 ENTAC 87
ML Aviation Company
    53
Montgomery, Gen Sir
    Bernard *66*, 76, *76*
Moseley, Captain E. 20
Mountbatten, Admiral
    Lord Louis 76

Navarre, General 77
New Guinea *33, 72, 74*
Nixon, Pres. Richard *97*
North Africa *12, 15-16,*
    23, *27,* 31, 33, 37,
    52, 59, 61-2, *63,*
    63-4
Nuffield Mechanizations
    Ltd

car 4x4 Airborne 52

Okinawa *73*

Pacific theater 33, *33,*
    45, *49, 72-5*
Panhard armed car 11
Patton, Gen George S. *5,*
    75, 76
Payne, Charles 17, 19, 21
Philippines *69*, 76, *77,*
    79
Porsche 4x4 amphibian
    13
Probst, Karl K. 19-20
Putnam, P.C. 70
Pyle, Ernie 45

Recoilless rifles *3*, 61, 86
Remagen Bridge 33
Reynolds, Senator R. 21
Ridgway, Gen Matthew
    82
Rikuo Company 13
rocket launchers *59*
rockets 60, 61
Rokossovsky, Marshal
    74
Rolls Royce Tender 11
Roosevelt, Pres. F.D. 76
Ross, Delmar J. 17, 21
Rzeppa company 29

Schmidt, Wilhelm 66
Segar, artist 23
Short, Gen Walter C. 17
Simpson, Gen William
    76
Skerrit, Tom 106
Skorzeny, Otto 65
Smart T25 armored jeep
    40
Soviet Army 52, 74
Soviet Union,
    GAZ 46 MAV 79
    GAZ 67 B *52-3*
    and Lend-Lease 22-3,
    47, 52
Sparkman and Stephens
    70
Spicer transmission
    company 17, 19, 29
Stephens Jr., Roderick
    70
Stilwell, Gen Joseph *71*
Stimson, Henry L. 21
Stirling, Lt Col David 61,
    62, 63, 64
Studebaker amphibian
    70
Suez Canal operation 86
Sutherland, Donald 106
Sutherland, General *69*

T 24 Scout Car 40
Tararine, Marc 71

Townsend, L/Cpl L.H.
    78
Toyota Company 13
Tracta Company 29
trailers 32-3, *58*, 58-9
Tunis, *16, 24-5, 28*

United States Air Force
    50-51
    81st Troop Carrier
    Group 31
    C-141 Starlifter *10*
United States Army,
    Continental Army
    Command 96
    Office of Production
    Management 22
    Ordnance Department
    15, 17, 18
    Quartermaster Corps
    18, 21-2
    and definitive
    specification 22
    Tank Destroyer
    Command 39
    5th Army *30*
    7th Army 61
    3rd Corps 37, *37*
    Corps of Signals *45*
    1st Infantry Div. *97*
    82nd Airborne Div. *43,*
    54
    101st Air Assault Div.
    109
    101st Airborne Div. *41*
    173rd Airborne Bde *3*
    16th Infantry Regt 66
    105th Medical Bn *36*
    644th Ordnance Coy 41
    and evolution of jeep
    15-20
    in France *2, 30,* 37
United States Army Air
    Force *49*
    81st Troop Carrier Sqdn
    47
United States Coast
    Guard 37, *49*
United States Marine
    Corps *25*, 45, 60,
    60, 61, 81, *91, 94-5,*
    99, 101
Up Front (Mauldin) 32

Vanderveen, Bart H. 13,
    71
Vietnam *97-9, 102*
Volkswagen
    Kubelwagen *12,* 13, 86
    Pkw Kfz. 1-4, 13
    Volkswagen 181 13
    166 Schwimmwagen 13

Wajda, Adrezj 106
Warner, Philip 47
Weeks, Col John 58

Weiss Company 29
Willys jeep *6-7,* 28
    CJ3A 100
    CJ3B 91, 93
    CJ5 (M606A2,
    M606A3) *9,* 91, 100
    CJ6 93
    M38 8, 98, 100
    M38A1 *9, 86-8,* 100-101
    variations of 100
    MB *9, 22,* 23, *43, 61, 66*
    4x4 Cargo 39
    MB-L Special (WAC)
    54

Quad *9,* 21, 22, *22*
    refinements to 23
Willys-Bombardier T28,
    T29 40-41
Willys-Overland Motors
    Inc. 17, 19, 20, 21,
    22, 87
Willys Overland (Brasil)
    91
Woolcombe, Robert 27
World War I 1, 11, 15
World War II 8, 11, 18,
    27-34, 37, 39-42,
    45, 47

Acknowledgments

The author and publisher would like to thank Ron Callow, the designer; Stephen Small, the editor; Rita Longabucco, the picture researcher; Nicki Giles and Veronica Price, for production; Ron Watson for preparing the index; and the individuals and institutions listed below for supplying the pictures:

Bison Books, pages: 84 (top), 85 (bottom), 97 (top)
National Archives of Canada, page: 40
Will Fowler, pages: 9 (top), 10 (top), 64 (top/British Aerospace), 88-9, 92-3, 100, 104-5
Ray Hutchins, pages: 56-7
Imperial War Museum, pages: 4, 11 (top), 12 (bottom), 14 (both), 15, 17, 18 (top), 20 (bottom/TRH), 29, 30 (top), 32, 33 (top/TRH and bottom), 36 (top), 37, 38 (both), 43 (both), 44 (top), 58, 59 (both), 62 (both), 63 (bottom), 65 (both), 66 (both), 67 (both), 71 (both), 74, 76 (bottom), 77 (bottom)
Israeli Government Press Office, pages: 84 (bottom), 85 (top), 86, 87
Reprinted by permission of Bill Mauldin and the Watkins/Loomis agency, page: 23 (both)
Andrew Morland, pages: 6-7, 10 (bottom), 53 (both), 61 (both)
The National Army Museum, pages: 63 (top)
Pictorial Press, pages: 16, 24-5, 26 (both), 27, 28, 39, 44 (bottom), 45, 77 (top right), 79, 90 (top), 108
Courtesy of Major William Reid, pages: 5, 8-9, 18 (bottom), 19, 20 (top), 21, 22 (both), 23, 48 (top), 52, 55 (bottom), 84 (top), 85 (bottom), 108
The Peter Roberts Collection, c/o Neill Bruce, pages: 49 (top and bottom)
U.S. Army, pages: 1 (TRH), 3 (TRH), 30-1, 34, 36 (bottom), 42, 48 (bottom), 68-9, 75 (top), 77 (top left), 83 (bottom), 99 (top/TRH)
U.S. Department of Defense, pages: 35 (both), 60, 73 (Will Fowler), 82 (TRH), 83 (top/TRH), 90 (bottom/TRH), 91, 94-5 (TRH), 96 (TRH), 98 (TRH), 99 (bottom/TRH), 101 (Will Fowler), 102 (both/TRH), 103 (TRH), 109
U.S. National Archives, pages: 41 (TRH), 50-1 (TRH), 54 (TRH), 55 (top/TRH), 72 (TRH), 75 (bottom/TRH), 70, 80-1
TRH, pages: 97 (bottom/Hughes Aircraft), 107 (both/E Neville), 110 (Y Debay)